Adult Faith

Adult Faith

Growing in
Wisdom and Understanding

Diarmuid O'Murchu, MSC

ORBIS BOOKS
Maryknoll, New York 10545

Founded in 1970, Orbis Books endeavors to publish works that enlighten the mind, nourish the spirit, and challenge the conscience. The publishing arm of the Maryknoll Fathers and Brothers, Orbis seeks to explore the global dimensions of the Christian faith and mission, to invite dialogue with diverse cultures and religious traditions, and to serve the cause of reconciliation and peace. The books published reflect the views of their authors and do not represent the official position of the Maryknoll Society. To learn more about Maryknoll and Orbis Books, please visit our website at www.maryknollsociety.org.

Library of Congress Cataloging-in-Publication Data

O'Murchu, Diarmuid.
    Adult faith : growing in wisdom and understanding / Diarmuid O'Murchu.
      p. cm.
    Includes bibliographical references (p.   ) and index.
    ISBN 978-1-57075-886-7 (pbk.)
    1. Life cycle, Human – Religious aspects – Christianity. 2. Maturation (Psychology) – Religious aspects – Christianity. 3. Adulthood. 4. Faith. I. Title.
BV4597.555.O47 2010
248.8'4 – dc22   2010010251

Contents

Introduction

When I was a child, I spoke like a child, I thought like a child, I reasoned like a child. When I became an adult, I gave up childish ways. —1 COR. 13:11

Being a loyal, docile member of a single tribal group does not offer salvation any longer, if ever it did. Now the world is in need of people who can feel several loyalties, several affinities, several identities. — NAOMI GOLDENBERG

WELL HIDDEN by surrounding bookcases, a young man indulged his turbulent spiritual search, immersed in a text that his professors had warned him was unsuitable, even dangerous material, for a clerical student. But he relished forbidden fruit, not because of the excitement of playing with danger, but because it was setting his soul on fire. In fact, it was going to change his outlook forever. The book he was reading was *The Divine Milieu* by Pierre Teilhard de Chardin; the year was 1970; and the reader, if you have not already guessed, was the author of this book.

As a young person I grew up and was educated in twentieth-century Catholic Ireland with a very distinctive indoctrination, based on a religion of fear, guilt, and unworthiness. Authority was absolute and the central doctrines of a ruling, controlling church, representing a harshly demanding God on high, dictated a very clear sense of right and wrong.

The church I knew was heavily influenced by what contemporary scholars call the imperial mind-set. Postcolonial studies clarify and expose the controlling dynamics of that paradigm. In my case, I was left in no doubt that I was a citizen of Ireland, that I belonged to the

Island of Saints and Scholars, who sent out missionaries to convert pagans all over the world and particularly the British Protestants, who were projected as the archenemies of every Irish person. Had I remained firmly rooted within that colonizing worldview I would probably still be holding on to it with a vengeance, as a small sector of my compatriots still do. But with the cultural irruptions of the 1960s and thereafter such ideologies became difficult to maintain.

In my case, three things began to shift my insular worldview.

1. The introduction of television into Ireland in the 1960s. Continuous exposure to the visual impact of a wider world, of other ways of seeing and understanding, created a subconscious mind-shift through which I became suspicious and began to question my inherited indoctrination.

2. My exposure to the writings of the priest palaeontologist Pierre Teilhard de Chardin in the 1970s, opening up a new spiritual and theological landscape, which began to blow apart the inherited tenets of my narrow inherited tradition.

3. Exposure to other cultures, with the progressive realization that my beloved island of "saints and scholars" was only a tiny dimension of a vast and wonderful universe. For me, this exposure was gradual, and did not involve extensive travel until the 1990s.

When I reflect on my own experience, I can identify some factors that contribute to a more flexible way of seeing and understanding our world. At a subconscious level, the information explosion (via television, Internet, cell phone, etc.) may well be the single greatest catalyst changing contemporary ways of seeing and understanding. Travel and exposure to other cultures contribute significantly, as does wider access to formal education, although this can also contribute to conceptual and intellectual rigidity.

There is another major factor, which much of the scholarly literature either ignores, overlooks, or subverts, namely, a shift in spiritual meaning. I was well into my twenties before I realized this was happening to me. By then I had already let go (outgrown) elements of the fear and dogmatism, so central to my faith in earlier years. More significantly, I had begun to think for myself, read more extensively, and explore questions of religious meaning, which a mere decade earlier I had not dared to do. With hindsight, I realize I had begun the long journey of living my faith *as an adult,* and outgrowing the more childlike dependent behaviors that had sustained me in earlier years.

The childlike — and often childish — beliefs no longer nourished, inspired, or challenged me. Appropriating an adult sense of faith, however, was an onerous task, with few blueprints to adopt and few trusted soul-mates to befriend during what (for me at least) was often a lonely and bewildering journey. Either sheer luck or grace-filled fortune (probably a mixture of both), kept me on track, until eventually I could name and articulate what was unfolding within my inner being. The process still continues, and like every organic development, will always remain an open-ended process.

Today millions are traveling this pilgrim route, yet few formal religions or churches acknowledge the phenomenon, and some vociferously denounce and malign it. This is a spiritual revolution from the ground up, and it is here to stay. Above all else it is an exploration into adult faith, as people become more adult in their foundational belief in life and seek an adult God to be their friend and guide on the way. I hope this book will prove to be a helpful resource for all traversing this exciting but daunting journey.

Structure of the Book

The book is written in two parts:

Part One is an attempt to deconstruct what has been inhibiting a more adult appropriation of our faith: the beliefs, dogmas, regulations and institutions that have been controlling us and keeping us in our place, but more importantly, the cultural and religious dynamics that facilitated what often feels like a codependent process.

Part Two is an attempt at reconstruction, seeking to honor and embrace two cultural developments of our time: first, a new way of defining what it means to be an adult person, with the ensuing implications for appropriating religious belief, and second, evolutionary factors that may be creating, or impacting upon, that new understanding of what it means to be human today.

Each chapter ends with three summary statements, which can be used as topics for discussion:

(a) ***Conventional inherited wisdom,*** and how it has kept people trapped and subdued in ways that have failed to honor their adulthood.

(b) ***Embedded codependency,*** a set of dynamics — often subtle and sometimes invisible — through which people have been kept in subjugation.

(c) ***Adult empowerment,*** the desires and aspirations now coming to the fore as people wish to be treated as mutually responsible adults.

Part One

The Vanishing Covenant

In that he says, a new covenant. He has made the first obsolete.
Now what is becoming obsolete and growing old is ready to
vanish away. — HEB. 8:13

C OPING WITH CHANGE is one of the most destabilizing experiences
for human beings. No matter how often we change house or
job, or make other major adjustments in life, change is still a daunting
challenge. And as we grow older it becomes more difficult. But young
people, also, can find it scary.

As we enter the twenty-first century the rapidity and enormity of
change increases all the time. This is particularly obvious in the realm
of information technology, with almost weekly breakthroughs for
faster output and novel strategies. There are also evolutionary driving forces, which most people are not familiar with — because our
standard education tends to ignore, and sometimes undermine, such
features.

In Part One of this book I review some of these changing features particularly in the cultural, social, and religious domains. Many
inherited patterns emphasized our dependence on others — wiser
and better than ourselves. Some were perceived to have made it,
and most of us never would. A subtle and pervasive codependency
had infiltrated every sphere of life, often endorsed by religion, education, economics, governance, and the cultural norms evolving from
those controlling powers. This is the old covenant rapidly losing its
relevance and credibility.

I invite the reader to embrace this painful letting go of a normative (occasionally, cherished) past, to be more aware of its gradual breakdown, along with the substantial resistances to such letting-go, and gracefully learn to grieve that which needs to die and fade into history. Since much of this transition is about power and status, it evokes strong negative reactions with a tendency to demonize those who try to engage more responsibly and creatively. Hopefully, the brief analysis I offer will empower people to handle these reactions and resistances with greater wisdom and integrity.

Chapter One

Defining Adulthood

FOCUS: An evolutionary shift is transpiring, from an individualistic functionary understanding of the human person to one that is more egalitarian, relational, and always in process.

Psychologists today use the term "emerging adulthood" to de-scribe a new phase in young adult experience. People in their twenties and early thirties recognize that they are no longer adolescents, but many see themselves as not yet adult.
— James and Evelyn Whitehead

WE TALK A LOT about people being *adult,* along with the chal-lenges and responsibilities that may be involved. Adulthood covers a spectrum of experiences with a vast range of adaptations in terms of behavior and lifestyle. Being an adult means a range of different things to different people. Most of us are so busy in the adult world, doing adult things, we rarely find time to stop and ask ourselves basic identity questions. Our roles and functions tend to dictate our becoming.

According to Aristotle's *Nicomachean Ethics* (book 1, chap. 7), the activity of *reasoning* is what makes you human (and therefore, adult) since no other living organism has the capacity for reasoning. The essence of being human is specified in the ability to use *the fac-ulty of reason.* According to Jean Piaget, our ability to figure things out, using the power of reason, matures during our teenage years and is assumed to be well developed by late adolescence. Chronolog-ically, this translates into reaching one's eighteenth birthday, the age adopted by most cultures for the right to vote and the expectation of *functioning as an adult* in society.

Many of these ideas are based on rather cerebral, metaphysical concepts. There is a tendency to quantify and identify specific time boundaries in which childhood ceases and adulthood begins. With the growth of developmental psychology throughout the twentieth century, we moved away from rigid, timeless categories and began to understand the entire life cycle in a more informed and nuanced way.

There is a great deal of evidence to substantiate Dr. Harry Blatterer (2007), who categorically asserts that it is the economic forces of capitalism, more than anything else, that determines and defines adulthood in contemporary society. The market sets what Blatterer calls "the classical markers of adulthood": independence, family and work. In practice this tripartite focus translates into: a job, heterosexual marriage, a mortgage, life insurance, children, the family car, superannuation, retirement plans, a will. And clearly his is the ideal to which the deprived half of humanity must also aspire.

Even in the Western, so-called developed nations, millions never reach this target. The attainment of adulthood presents a much more complex picture. In terms of educational achievement, skills acquisition, professional competence, and the ability to contribute to society in the capacity of a formal wage earner, most people reach adulthood by age twenty-five or thereabouts. By this same time, the ability to function socially is well in place through a range of friendships, work-related acquaintances, and in some cases, one or more serious couple relationships. It is the psychological dynamics, and their articulation, that throw up a whole new set of challenges for mature growth in the intellectual, social, emotional, and spiritual dimensions of human life. It is the integration of these various elements that characterizes the evolution of adult maturity.

From the time of the classical Greeks till the mid-twentieth century, psychological growth (studied mainly by philosophers) pertained primarily to the formation of character in children and adolescents. Early childhood set in place blueprints that would remain unchanged for the rest of one's life. (Freud delved much deeper than the philosophers.) And it was widely assumed that human character was fully formed by late adolescence; what you were then is what you would remain for the rest of your life.

As long as one functioned effectively in human society, it was assumed that adulthood was healthy and flourishing. For men, this meant the ability to do productive labor, earn a living wage, father children, and maintain control. For women, it meant becoming a wife and mother and attending to the needs of the home and childrearing. Living a fruitful and productive life is essentially what adulthood was about, a form of cultural acquiescence in which you played the expected role determined by the prevailing politics, economics, and religion of the time.

This is a form of adulthood heavily infiltrated with compromise and passivity. The responsible adult was the one who played by the rules of the game. You knew your place and did not deviate. In fact, millions did deviate, but were often subjugated or contained by the prevailing and unquestioned cultural norms. Only a relatively small elite enjoyed the freedom and support to advance in either knowledge or achievement. A kind of blandness characterized the culture of adult stature.

A Cultural Shift

The 1960s was a decade of cultural shift on a much bigger scale than formerly known. It is popularly associated with young people breaking loose from the more conventional ways of living known to previous generations. Many of those who evolved the "new age" culture, however, were folks in their twenties and thirties. Youth stretched well into the twenties or thirties and sometimes beyond. One could argue that this was a revolution more about the transition into adulthood, rather than the departure from adolescence. Previous boundaries were blurred, and the cut-off point between adolescence and adulthood became particularly fluid and fuzzy. It continues to be open and fluid today.

Much more significant was the emotional breakthrough. Feelings, moods, and emotions were no longer for the private domain. The primacy of rationality was dethroned, brutally at times; it is still struggling to recover. An archetypal power seemed to be reawakening, and the adult who previously lived by the expectations of reason and rationality now sought an expanded horizon that defied the conventional wisdom that had prevailed during previous centuries.

Adulthood was being redefined — and in fact still is — which the message of this book clearly verifies. The American psychiatrist Robert J. Lifton (1999) popularized the notion of the *protean self,* an expanded sense of personal identity that was already in vogue in the 1970s (see Becker 1971; Kennedy 1974). Instead of a clear-cut fixed identity, with biological significance very much to the fore, the protean tends to manifest a more fluid multiple personality, with the added ability to morph into a range of differing identities as complex demands arise. It is not so much a case of developing new skills to cope with a rapidly changing environment. Rather the evolving environment is evoking new potentials, redefining the very essence of what it means to be human. (I'll return to the notion of the protean self in chapter 8.)

This is *coevolution* at work. A frequently noted example is the dexterity of eye and hand with which teenagers play computer games. While the protean is externalized more vividly in youth, I propose that its materialization in the adult happens more in the internal realm. Adults often don't catch up with this new evolutionary transformation until they reach older years (Fowler's universalizing stage; see below pp. 114–15). Only then can they break loose from the excessively rational conditioning of the dominant culture and begin to honor (and explore) what is really going on in their lives. No longer preoccupied with the daily burden of holding a regular job, paying off a mortgage, rearing a family, and devoting energy to the cultural distractions that bombard us each day, they begin to stand back, enter a more reflective space, and ask deeper questions.

Sometimes the questions have been surfacing for years, questions concerning the meaning of their work, religion, relationships, responsibilities. Only now in retirement does it feel safe enough to entertain their persistence and take a risk that might involve changes in life-direction that just felt too scary at an earlier time. The protean adult has been seeking attention for a long time; this new daring truth can no longer be suppressed.

Toward a New Integration

The foundational elements defining our humanity remain essentially the same across time and culture. The process of integration differs in accordance with evolutionary progress; new potentialities are evoked to engage with each new evolutionary breakthrough. The intellectual needs of a twentieth-century computer programer are certainly different from those of a person who lived five thousand years before the present time, or even from a person who lived a hundred years ago. On the other hand, we cannot always generalize as easily as that. When we review the artistic skills of the middle Palaeolithic Era we seem to be witnessing an integration of art and spirituality not as extensively in evidence in our time.

One also wonders how widely we appreciate and acknowledge the complex and diverse make-up of the human personality. Our ancient ancestors were probably not consciously aware of the psychological insights we possess today. Subconsciously they may have intuited their significance and integrated them in ways that defy our modern lifestyles. We who are aware do not seem to evoke this wisdom in our educational and developmental programs, which is often what militates against the evolution of the adult in contemporary life, and particularly in the realm of faith and religion.

The following six dimensions characterize human growth and the potential for the attainment of adulthood, across time and culture: the biological, the social, the emotional, the intellectual, the spiritual and the psychic. It is precisely the fresh appropriation of these dimensions that constitutes adult growth and development today. The goal of this endeavor seems to be something akin to a deeper integration of the various elements outlined above. To begin with, each merits a brief description:

The Biological

From birth to death every person goes through a process of biological and physical maturity. Millions just take it for granted and pay little attention until sickness or accident limits our physical ability. Few seem to be aware of the fact that one's biological organism thrives on change: every cell in the human body dies and is replaced every seven years. Without this unceasing process of birth–death–rebirth we would cease to be. Strictly speaking our biological constitution is a *process* and not a *product*.

Today, we are encouraged to listen more attentively to our bodies and take a more direct responsibility for the wholesome growth of our embodied selves. A great deal of unnecessary pain and suffering arise from neglect of our bodies, obesity being one of the more obvious examples; various forms of cancer and coronary problems are frequently linked with the unhealthy treatment of our bodies. Millions live away from the body, unconsciously compensating through fashionable clothing, excessive glamorizing of the body, or a range of compulsive substitutes such as gambling, drugs, or sex. Coming home to our bodies is a major challenge for adult advancement at this time. The spiritual challenges are formidable and will be reviewed throughout the chapters of this book.

The Social

We tend to underestimate the place of human friendship, not merely in terms of human growth, but also as a process through which we engage with life and make valuable contributions to the growth and development of human society. Many valuable friendships are fractured and strained by the competitive driving forces of modern life. The tendency to use friendship for utilitarian purposes has also increased enormously in recent decades; we make friends, not merely for the sake of friendship, but to enhance our hopes to make progress in life.

In our age of ecological corespondibility, the circle of care and friendship needs to extend to the nonhuman world as well. Previously, we experienced this through favorite pets, while those who worked the land innately knew this deeper sense of connection and conviviality. Adult sociality today calls for a new sense of inclusiveness: beyond our cherished human friends, are the millions who are victimized by oppression and exclusion, and the earth itself is barbarized and exploited to serve human greed. The new sociability needs to embrace all these dimensions.

The Emotional

In the domain of rational discourse, feeling and emotion are suspect. The pursuit of objectivity tends to ignore, and often subverts, the wisdom of emotional insight. Educationally, we are not well equipped to deal with our emotions, to listen to them, interpret them, and learn from them. Religions tend to moralize a great deal about strong emotions, especially anger, jealousy, and sexual feelings, and consequently, we often miss the inspiring wisdom they embody and convey (see Whitehead and Whitehead 2009).

Many popular webpages, on features or characteristics of adulthood, suggest that our strong feelings need to be tamed and brought under the bar of reason. Throughout this book, I emphasize *integration* rather than *taming*. One of the unique features of adult development is the ability to empower oneself and others through a more integrated appropriation of feelings and emotions. For the adult, anger is not merely a wrong to get rid of. It is a powerful passion, activating an empowering energy. We need to listen to it, befriend it, engage with it, and transform its energy in the direction of mutuality and justice-making. Jealousy is not just a childish projection, but an inner voice of longing, a painful desiring, needing gentle attention, discernment, and the courage to assume the healing and empowerment for which inner wisdom is crying out.

The Intellectual

Gross confusion exists between *intellectual* and *academic* achievement. Every person is blessed with intellect, with its accompanying desire to comprehend and understand more deeply. Many adults use their intellect in highly creative and responsible ways, but often receive little acknowledgment or credit.

Our world is addicted to academic achievement, which in itself guarantees neither the development of intellect nor the wisdom that is required to live intelligently in the world. Academic achievement is grossly overrated, and those unable to rise to that level often are relegated to menial tasks and dismissive judgment. The integration of our intellectual wisdom is a primary challenge for adult faith development in the twenty-first century. It will be a recurring theme throughout the pages of this book.

The Spiritual

This is one of the most neglected spheres of human growth and development, particularly for adults. It is widely assumed that our spiritual sphere is nurtured through the appropriation and practice of a particular religion. There is a tendency in all the great religions to pass on religious wisdom through doctrines and creeds, with emphasis on knowing the verbal formulations. Adults are judged to be religious if they can pass on those beliefs to future generations just as they have been passed on to them. But this transmission is often lacking in internalized understanding; the neophyte learns the formula, and frequently is unable to apply it to daily life in an integrated way.

The bigger challenge is the realization that we are all endowed with an inner transparency for the holy, for the mystery we popularly call "God." We are programed internally in the power of living spirit, always inviting us to attune more deeply to the Great Spirit who infuses the whole of creation. Whether we adopt a religion or not, we are innately spiritual and will remain so throughout our entire lifespan. For contemporary adults, this awareness is quite widespread and is raising formidable challenges for the meaning and place of formal religion in human living.

The Psychic

This is the creative energy that enables us to work toward the integration of all the other dimensions outlined above. In theological language this is the energizing power of the Holy Spirit of God. In scientific language, it is the field force that activates and sustains all the other field influences through which we thrive and flourish.

Quantum physics is the reservoir of knowledge through which we can best understand this all-encompassing dimension. It is the whole that is always greater than the sum of the parts, that compelling "more" that lures both the mystic and martyr to greater depths, as brilliantly articulated in Winter (2009). It is the restlessness in the human heart that can never be fully satisfied and yet forever seeks articulation and mediation. It is the greatness in the human spirit that so often inspires and challenges us. For the adult person of faith, it is the horizon that forever beckons us toward new vistas of meaning and possibility.

Therefore, the concept of the "adult," as used throughout this book, is not merely about somebody who has reached the age of "maturity," nor merely somebody who is capable of Piaget's processes of formal operations. It involves a great deal more than undertaking an active civil role in society. It embraces a lifelong, evolving process rather than something attained at a certain stage in the life cycle. More importantly, it is a relational dynamic engaging life at different levels from the large-scale cosmic dimension to one's interdependent interaction with life's tiniest organisms at the subatomic level. And it is about a certain quality of interaction and participation, with *integration* as the primary goal. In a word, adulthood is attained — more accurately approximated — when a wholesome *integration* is being pursued in my engagement with all of life's demands upon me from the cosmic to subatomic (cellular) levels of reality.

The Enlarged Context

The need to redefine our notion of adulthood itself arises from the evolutionary changes happening in the world we inhabit. Ours is a time of major transitions, and many are happening at a lightning pace. In all cases we see a new sense of expansiveness. Everything is being stretched; context is being enlarged; the search for meaning requires multidisciplinary understandings.

Of singular importance is the recontextualization of the human within the cosmic, planetary, and ecological spheres of life. Gone is the day for viewing the human in isolation, nor can we any longer indulge in the inflation of the human addiction to power and domination. Not merely is the damage to the environment immoral, the threat to the human species itself is becoming all too obvious. The new adulthood seeks a more benign and sustainable relationship with the entire web of life. This may well be the greatest integration awaiting our attention and commitment. And it presses upon us with great urgency.

To facilitate the breakthrough we first need to examine those cultural metanarratives that hold ourselves and our planet to ransom. Although many of the older ways of operating are fragmenting, losing cultural significance, and failing to animate and inspire, they still hold a rigid grip on our consciousness and our ways of behaving. In Part One of this book, I name them briefly in the hope of raising the consciousness to address their demise proactively rather than with cynicism and reaction. The metanarratives I have in mind include the following:

- the concept of the nation-state;
- the revealed truth of formal religion;
- the Keynesian basis for modern economics;
- patriarchal power structures;
- the ideology of fierce competition;
- the commodification of earth's resources;
- Aristotelian-driven individualism;
- the valorization of rational thought.

These, too, are among the chief factors undermining the evolution of more authentic adulthood in our time. Each will be reviewed briefly in the chapters that follow.

Doing justice to this complex emergence is not easy. Those committed to safeguarding the dominant, functional reality of former times (and still prevalent today) will feel very threatened by the new, while those embracing the new have little or no interest in retaining the old. While striving to update those committed to the older ways, which they claim have stood the test of time, we could easily lose the new seekers completely. I will attempt a compromise: *be brief on that which is fading into historical memory, and give the greater attention to that which will eventually engage us all.* And that precipitation is likely to emerge more rapidly than we think.

(a) **Conventional inherited wisdom** *required adults to be robust, self-reliant individuals who could manage reality in a controlled way and teach others to do the same.*

(b) **Embedded codependency** *resulted in the few — mainly males — attaining true adulthood, and everybody else was consigned to passive dependency as in a conventional parent-child arrangement.*

(c) **Adult empowerment** *involves a shift of developmental focus from the child/adolescent to the adult, along with whole new ways of seeing and understanding what adulthood is about in these coevolutionary times.*

Chapter Two

Ruling in Order to Control

FOCUS: Governance as exercised across the contemporary world is an inherited patriarchal strategy, based on a top-down chain of command. It is inherently disempowering for the majority of humankind, and for most people it seriously undermines their development as adult selves.

I am puzzled that a species that has subjected virtually the entire universe to its analytical gaze and that has penetrated to the tiniest constituents of matter still knows next to nothing about how to become human. — WALTER WINK

HUMAN ADULTHOOD is stymied by the very institutions we deem essential to upholding the rights and dignity of people. Even in so-called democratic countries, power is held in the hands of the few, leaving the majority feeling powerless most of the time. We elect governments and relish the power of being able to do so. But in between elections, we enjoy little say and less power in what actually transpires. Parliamentarians enjoy many so-called democratic rights, but not those who have voted them into power.

The right to vote is a token gesture to keep people subdued. In most cases it does not empower toward democratic participation, for the greater part of the citizenry of democratic countries are passive onlookers. Not surprisingly, growing numbers of people become disillusioned and disenchanted. Increasingly, for younger citizens this is likely to lead to the violence that arises from apathy and frustration. Public property and public representatives of the system, e.g., police, become targets for the subconscious anger and disempowerment.

Democratic Disempowerment

About 2 billion people — almost one in every three — still live in oppressive political regimes. Even where freedom is tolerated, as in China, surveillance of human conduct is intense, and for the slightest deviations punishment can be harsh and extreme. The remaining two-thirds of humanity enjoy democratic governance, variously defined and implemented through a wide range of political structures. Where democratic governance prevails, people have the right to choose governments and dispose of them when dissatisfied. However, democracy is a veneer, embodying numerous problematic features.

Even the most democratic of contemporary governments have adopted a patriarchal orientation virtually unassailable in modern consciousness. Democratic governance is not just a mode of political organization on behalf of people. It is also an inherited ideology based on complex power agendas — favoring those who have the power to gain even more power, to the advantage of a limited few.

According to current cultural norms, most humans require designated individuals and organizations to manage reality on their behalf. Humans are perceived as essentially codependent creatures whose affairs need to be managed and controlled by designated leaders. In a word, the adult maturity of most people is neither acknowledged nor promoted in the contemporary political consciousness.

An active-passive dualism dominates the entire system. A more egalitarian sharing of power cannot be seriously entertained. The fear of chaos and anarchy looms large. The authority of those who govern and the obedience of those who are governed are the linchpins of the entire system. Not merely do a tiny minority of humankind own most of the wealth; they also own most of the power. The dire consequences of this imbalance became all too real in the worldwide recession of the early twenty-first century. The welfare of the entire species was thrown into jeopardy by the reckless behavior of financial "wildcats" whose behavior in some cases was tolerated, and even supported, by mainline governments.

The Historical Backdrop

To understand the complex nature of this system, we need to visit its historical grounding. Scholarly analysts tend to evade or explain away the inherited dysfunctionality. Fully fledged "democracy" — through the mechanism of the nation-state — evolved in the sixteenth century, and this is as far back as many political analysts are prepared to look. Some will trace the origins to classical Greek times and the inherited texts of Plato and Aristotle. We need a more radical naming of sources, particularly *the primordial patriarchal foundations* that our contemporary academic world considers too obscure to trace. Is it obscurity or fear of radical exposure?

Few disciplines seriously consider the major cultural shifts accompanying the agricultural revolution some five thousand to eight thousand years ago. It resulted in new divisions of land and territory, with what seems to be a largely, if not totally, new system of governance and administration. Inspiring this new regime was the religious force that was understood to control and guide everything on earth. This was the sky-God, the divine ruler who reigned from above the clouds. It was a male God, assumed to be of kingly status, one who governed with the absolute authority associated with earthly monarchs.

This divine power from on high was mediated through the king on earth. The king (not the priest or shaman) was considered to be the primary representative of God on earth. The king himself was often deemed to be divine. Roman emperors frequently invoked this divine status, requiring subjects at times to address them with designations such as "Son of God." Echoes of the divine right of kings still reverberate in the modern world, e.g., in Thailand, Japan, and the UK.

Presumably, it is against this background that Aristotle postulated that those in governance are *always* just and should be regarded as such. No matter how corrupt or irresponsible they are, we must give them the benefit of the doubt. If they are of God and represent divine power on earth, they mirror and reflect the divine's concern for humanity. Sounds like blind faith mediated through blind obedience!

To our contemporaries many of these ideas sound archaic, even ridiculous. Such ideas endure precisely because they have mutated into an ideology that has often been religiously validated and politically canonized. Despite corruption and the gross abuse of power, few people are prepared to question seriously the foundations of what we know. The system has us exactly where it wants us: passive, compliant creatures who don't think too deeply, won't ask penetrating questions, and certainly won't shake the foundations of our dominant institutions.

But time is running out! The young are opting out at an accelerating pace, and many are not prepared to tolerate any longer what they long took for granted. We need alternatives to the prevailing system. While this is apparent to growing numbers of people, only a tiny minority are ready to opt for such alternatives. The risk feels enormous to most people. Faced with this dilemma, many seem to adopt the stance that "the devil you know is better than the one you do not know."

Similar power dynamics were played out in the financial crisis of the opening decades of the twenty-first century. The U.S. president, Barack Obama, described as shameful and irresponsible the behavior of leading bankers in the United States. Had the crisis not hit us, nobody would have denounced such greedy power. Some think it is an inevitable dimension of all big businesses. I suggest it is the hidden, festering poison in all patriarchal systems. This inherited tradition is inherently corrupt and pervasively disempowering for most people.

The Patriarchal Inheritance

The reign of patriarchy is so endemic to contemporary cultures that few feel any need to evaluate or question it. Even feminist critics hold varying views on how we define the issue and how we might set out to rectify it. There are overt and covert dimensions needing urgent attention. Overtly, patriarchy translates into ways of governing and managing resources — human and otherwise — adopting a strategy of control from the top down. Such power belongs primarily to those who have earned the right to exercise control, but not necessarily the most competent or intelligent for this undertaking. Patriarchal management is first and foremost about power, not about intelligence or skill.

The power in question is power over, the need for some to manage and control the affairs of others, a strategy based on some key assumptions of a highly questionable nature:

+ People are fickle and prone to "evil" and, therefore, need to be controlled; things could get badly out of hand if this were not the case.

+ The planet is a material object for human use and benefit; we need responsible human management of its resources.

+ The resources of creation are limited (scarce), so we need to be clear on who has the right to regulate the use of resources and who must subject themselves to such regulation.

+ Fierce competition, but carefully regulated by those who know best, seems to be the approach that has proved its worth over time.

Such convictions evoke anger and ridicule from growing numbers of the human species. Living as we do in a world of mass information, millions no longer trust those who seek to govern and control. We know that such theoretical foundations are seriously flawed. Intuitively we sense that things could be different and will need to be for a more promising future. Culturally, a big part of our dilemma is that we cannot as yet muster the creativity and cultural consensus to generate alternative ways of relating to life and to one another.

So the human species finds itself in a quite a dilemma. Philosophers blame much of the problem on the phenomenon known as *postmodernism,* where humans deprived of a central metanarrative are at the mercy of conflictual vested interests with greed and individualism running amok. I suggest that postmodernism is a symptom rather than a cause of the underlying problem. Indeed, the collapse of leading metanarratives may be our greatest sign of hope.

For much of the twentieth century we knew only one metanarrative, one foundational truth embodied in those who governed: those in charge know best. Why? Because according to the leading narrative, God designed it that way. Aristotle claimed that those in governance are *automatically* just. Even when they behave outrageously, we must still respect and obey them. No longer will people accept this, politically, economically, socially, or even ecclesiastically — although millions among the deprived and impoverished have little choice other than going along with the prevailing system. Religion is one of the few institutions left where blind obedience still exerts quite an influence; many people believe that churches and religions really are of God, and, despite some glaring contradictions, they still convey the truth of God.

The Breakdown...

We need an evolutionary perspective to comprehend what is transpiring at this time. We need a big picture so that we can discern against a larger and deeper background. We also need a spirituality that can entertain and embrace paradox (Moore 2004; Tickerhoof 2002; Winter 2009); in times of major transition — culturally, politically, socially — paradox abounds, and its contradictory nature is more baffling and disturbing.

A time of breakdown is also a time for *grieving*. We need to mourn the loss of those systems and institutions that served us well in the past, but are no longer capable of doing so. Without this grieving, we can all too easily get stuck in our grief and cannot liberate ourselves to let go of the old and embrace the new.

For Westerners, particularly, this is a daunting task. We repress grief and loss with layers of denial and repression, and we have been doing it for a long time. Our inability to handle personal grieving — our basic lack of know-how — is a serious handicap in a world where institutional and systemic breakdown is so widespread. Unable to handle the cultural and systemic need to grieve, we resort to the safety net of the old, despite the fact that we know intuitively that many of the former models are in an advanced stage of terminal decline.

This cultural fragmentation, and our unreadiness to grieve the loss, throw our adult-selves into confusion and anomie. Regression to the safety and security that the child within every one of us seeks tends to run deeper (largely unconscious, of course). And we will find plenty of distractions and allurements to dull our inner pain, *shopping* being to the fore at the present time. Remember what George Bush advised the American people a few days after September 11, 2001: maintain their regular shopping behaviors! Not much adult challenge or inspiration in that advice!

Those who see the deeper picture, those who raise different questions, and the few who venture to disagree and ask for alternative ways of doing things, these are the adults in our midst, the ones who offer a more realistic sense of hope for a different and better future. But faced with so much discomfort, even when it feels calamitous, we don't like those people who raise new adult prospects. That evokes even deeper feelings of insecurity, a painful reminder that many among us have not grown up and are still stymied at the level of infantile fear. This is the murky and painful landscape, which psychologists describe as *codependency*.

Our Codependent Culture

Frequently throughout this book I use the term "codependency," or the accompanying adjective, "codependent." Melody Beattie (1987; 2009) has popularized the concept of codependency in self-help literature (Starker 2002). She offers this definition for the lay reader: "A co-dependent person is one who has let another person's behavior affect him or her, and who is obsessed with controlling that person's behavior" (Beattie 1987, 36). The term became associated with behavior patterns frequently observed within families where alcohol addiction was a serious issue. The inability or unwillingness to confront the abusive drinker, the tendency to protect his or her destructive behavior, the need to be the other person's protector, the felt need to be wanted and needed, are all common symptoms of codependency.

Codependent behavior patterns are often inadvertently passed on from generation to generation. Barbara Fiese and Douglas Scaturo (1995) conducted group discussions with adult children of alcoholics (ACOAs) in an effort to understand the difficulties that they confront in parenting their children, given their own problematic upbringings. Internalizing the jargon used in treatment centers — excessive use of terms like "codependency," "pathological," "addiction," etc. — seemed to prevent group members from communicating with one another in clear, plain, easily understood language.

The treatment of codependent family dynamics is considerably more complex than the lay concept of codependency might suggest. Scaturo and his colleagues (2000) have discussed complexities in the family treatment of codependency that require a precise understanding and knowledge of the concept. Yet in practice that is difficult to attain, and the skill to work with the ensuing confusion can be surprisingly fruitful. Indeed, some would suggest that being at ease with this more open-ended way of working is itself a characteristic of adult confidence and maturity.

Codependency has something of a checkered history in psychology. It is not listed in the *DSM-IV-TR* diagnostic manual. I find the popular description of it being *a Messiah-complex* quite helpful. The need to exercise control and a subconscious fear of things being out of control are central dynamics in codependent relationships. These are also the dynamics that are often noted in imperial cultures and in the exercise of patriarchal governance, the intricacies of which are the focus of a relatively recent field of study known as *postcolonialism* (see p. 32 below).

Naming, confronting, and changing dysfunctional conduct is integral to the work of adult faith development. In codependent behavior, adulthood tends to be seriously compromised. In the modern world, we encounter large-scale failure in dealing with the adult in each other — in a respectful and empowering way. Parent-child games are played out in a range of disempowering ways, as insights from Transactional Analysis illustrate.[1]

Anarchy Let Loose?

Current modes of government are highly bureaucratic, costly to run, and even in the most advanced democracies leave many people feeling disempowered and undervalued. At least half of humanity does not enjoy democratic freedom in any real sense. It does not take a great stretch of the imagination to see that human governance, as exercised on planet earth at this time, leaves a great deal to be desired, and millions see little hope of reform being activated or initiated from within the existing institutions.

As often happens in the history of human affairs, there may not be a logical resolution. Ironically, extinction is often the only meaningful solution. Systems reach a stage of entrenchment and stagnation whereby they cannot be changed by human endeavor — the resistance is too deeply rooted — and the only possibility for forward movement is to let the system die out. To many this sounds like a morbid acquiescence, a kind of hopelessness that seems to betray everything that is noble in the human psyche. Without an informed culture of grieving, this sense of loss will not even be entertained, never mind embraced.

Systems theory is helpful to understand what is transpiring. All systems follow the scientific principle of the whole being greater than the sum of its parts. And systems govern many aspects of our daily lives. In terms of its psychic dynamics, a couple is a system, and not merely two individual organisms. One can know a great deal about each of the two individuals, and yet other things about their couple-behavior may defy rational explanation. The couple in itself is a living organism, and the success of its endeavor as a couple depends on how skilful each member is at dealing, not just with the other "half" but with the third organism called the *couple-relationship*. In marital counseling, the crucial skill rests in the counselor's ability to work with the *relationship* rather than with the two individual members.

Systemic wisdom, analysis, and insight are now needed to make sense of the dysfunctional systems (institutions) that influence, and often control, human behavior today. Many of the major institutions

that influence our daily lives — governmental, religious, social, political, economic — serve us poorly. They tend to keep us at a low level
of minimal survival, and we collude on a massive scale, because that
is how we have been indoctrinated. And we have been reminded all
too often that if we did not have the present dispensation, anarchy
would break loose and millions of people would be disenfranchised.
But millions are already disenfranchised, and billions of dollars are
spent each day to keep anarchy at bay.

So, the frustration cannot break out, which effectively leaves only
one other option: *break down!* The fragmentation is becoming much
more transparent, driving some to frustration and to new levels of
acted-out rage and anger, others to hedonistic individualism ("I'll
look after myself, to hell with everybody else"), and a minority to
what I suggest is a more mature "adult" response: let the system
die, and meanwhile let's put our energy into dreaming alternative
ways to move forward. The latter is not an easy option because it
inevitably evokes fear, defensiveness, and the scapegoating of the
prophetic voice itself.

This chapter seeks to highlight the critical power issues that confront us at this time and the systemic disempowerment that is still to
the fore in our human world. Most people do not realize anything
like their full adult potential. Most of the time we are condemned
to codependency in one or another of its several domesticated forms.
God never intended us to live this way, and the injustice of this dysfunctional mode is coming home to roost as more and more people
register their disapproval, or at least their unrest. The prevailing patriarchal system will continue to be upended, despite all the efforts of
the powers that be to maintain the status quo. As we move deeper into
the twenty-first century, the rehabilitation of the adult will continue
to shift the prevailing consciousness.

(a) **Conventional inherited wisdom** *can be encapsulated in one
key statement: the patriarchal mode of governance from the
top downward has stood the test of time, because among other
things, it is divinely instituted. Without it, anarchy would reign
supreme.*

(b) **Embedded codependency** *is the indoctrination that no alternative dispensation is worthy of consideration, nor must any be allowed to be seriously entertained.*

(c) **Adult empowerment** *involves the courage and wisdom to think differently — think outside the box, conjure up alternative schemes and models, and risk even life itself in order to give birth to a new paradigm that will honor the vision and creativity of adulthood.*

Chapter Three

The Religion of Fearful Submission

FOCUS: The prevailing patriarchal system, even in its secular expressions, is heavily endorsed by formal religion, which in all cases is based on belief in a male divinity ruling from on high, requiring a type of submission that is not conducive to adult empowerment.

All around us, we can see men and women throwing off their stereotypical roles, refusing to be the slaves of assigned identities.
— THEODORE ROSZAK

THE URGE TO DOMINATE and control, explored in the last chapter, owes much of its validity to formal religion. All formal religions highlight the central role of a governing deity. The divine one is assumed to be omnipotent, all powerful and all-wise, the corollary being that humans are totally dependent on the ruling deity.

In our inferior state, we can do nothing for ourselves. Only in the power of the Holy One who governs from on high can we live responsibly, and that has consequences not merely for this life but for the hereafter. Disobedience toward the Holy Power is the greatest crime of all, one that could earn you eternal damnation and perpetual estrangement in the life to come.

Love and Power Confused

Every religion, with the possible exception of Buddhism, believes in a God of unconditional love. That is the theory. That is what all the great scriptures claim. Orthodoxy out and out! Yet that is not what first springs to mind when people think about faith or religion. In most cases, mention of God and faith evokes fear, passivity, unworthiness, and the kind of codependency that images God as a parental figurehead, in the face of which children must know their place and keep it.

Unconditional love is an ideal that defies explanation or analysis, yet there is something in the very statement that resonates deep within every human being. At some stage in most of our lives we have known something verging on this noble ideal. Frequently, it has to do with those undramatic moments in which we encountered sheer goodness in another, perhaps in a gesture of care or concern, perhaps in a word of reassurance (and the word meant so much), perhaps in the silent presence of the one who was with us in deep solidarity, the magic touch at our low times of anguish and pain. Fortunately, many of us have had the experience, albeit fleetingly, and no words can really describe what it feels like.

When we refer to God's unconditional love, we are not describing a rationally known quality of the Holy One, nor are we regurgitating a creedal statement — because none exists to describe the indescribable. And let's not rush in with some threadbare psychological theories, claiming that people are merely projecting onto God from the depth of their own unworthiness and spiritual passivity. From Nietzsche, Feuerbach, Freud, and Durkheim in the 1800s down to Christopher Hitchens and Richard Dawkins in the twenty-first century, we have evidenced the demolition of projections and in all cases we failed to see that projections can also embody subconscious aspirations that cannot be dismissed rationally.

Attributions related to the unconditional love of God tend to arise from a deep resonance within ourselves where we intuitively know that something akin to sheer goodness does exist in our world. Partially, it is an inherited wisdom, one of great age, probably most deeply integrated in our ancient ancestors through their organic conviviality with creation in which their lives and values were embedded (see O'Murchu 2008).

Today there prevails a great deal of confusion between *the power of love* and *the love of power.* The latter has seriously undermined the former. The reassurance of unconditional love, which more than anything else empowers toward growth and maturity, is not available to many people in their daily experience. The culture of fierce competition, the resentments and jealousies involved in trying to make it to the top, undermine, and even ridicule, a culture of caring and mutual empowerment. Even in intimate relations, love struggles to hold its true place.

Problematic Religion

It is religion itself, more than any other cultural force, that has undermined and damaged the universal conviction of God's unconditional love. And in this process formal religion frequently robs people of their more adult insight into how the divine works in our midst. The reader may wish to retort and remind me that I am ignoring all the good that religion has achieved, serving as a wisdom that brings order, meaning, encouragement, a sense of community, and in some parts of the world religion has been a primary agent in providing health care, education, and social services. Yes, religion has achieved a great deal, but, I submit, within a systemic framework that has become highly problematic. The framework tends to create codependency rather than the liberation and empowerment that all the great scriptures claim to deliver.

There are four shadow elements that feature strongly in all the major religions:

1. The Patriarchal Foundation

The leading God figures in all the major faiths we know today tend to be imaged as mighty ruling kings, governing from a superior position above and outside this sinful, flawed world. The cultural paradigm of patriarchal power has been, and still is, so much taken for granted that many people fail to recognize its grip on human consciousness. In a system buttressed by subtle and sophisticated norms and institutions, we are heavily indoctrinated into thinking that this is the one and only way to operate in the world, that this is God's clear-cut choice for governance, both religious and secular, and that there is not, and never can be, any serious alternative.

This subtle but pervasive ideology is what is being identified in a relatively recent field of study known as postcolonialism. "Postcolonialism" loosely designates a set of theoretical approaches that focus on the direct effects and aftermaths of colonization, noting particularly how the colonizing influence is expressed in forms of human exploitation, normalization, repression, and dependency (see Said 1993; Bhabha 1994; Segovia and Sugirtharajah 2009). For instance, numerous postcolonial elements prevail in the way we teach history: the normalization and validation of violence, the priority of the ruling male, making the loser invisible, prioritizing the metaphor of the hero, concealing what we don't want the people to perceive. Internalized oppression is one of the more pervasive consequences of the colonial mind-set.[2]

Patriarchal cultures are adept at weakening anticipated challenge or opposition by inculcating guilt and unworthiness in those proposing alternative views of reality. People are made to feel guilty, unworthy, and disloyal. People are portrayed as betraying not merely the earthly authority but also the divine one. Correspondingly, suffering and sickness may be exalted as a compensation for sin and disobedience; our weakness helps to make us humble and therefore easier to control. Adult people of faith abhor these sinister strategies and the deviant spirituality that often accompanies such demeaning and disempowering colonization.

2. A Flawed Creation

To enforce even further the unquestioned power of the governing and controlling elite, creation itself is declared to be fundamentally flawed, a corrupt state for which religions offer a range of different explanations. In all cases a subtle (in Christianity, overt) anthropocentrism dominates the plot: humans are essentially corrupt; therefore creation must be. Humans are deemed to be totally in control of the material creation, an object to be used as humans see fit.

The theory of the fundamental flaw (original sin) is itself flawed all over. Both the underlying anthropology and the cosmology are seriously distorted. The story of God's elegant creation is reduced to a mere human artifact, at the mercy of crude ego inflation, which is the inflated imperialism of patriarchy itself. And having got itself into a bizarre double-bind, patriarchy must now extricate its tortured self. Inevitably it will do so by creating even more torture — and theories of violent redemption.

It will seek a scapegoat — in fact numerous scapegoats, a development brilliantly critiqued by the French theorist René Girard. Critiqued, but not well resolved, as Girard himself succumbs to the short-sightedness of the patriarchal mode, drawing most if not all his evidence from the patriarchal period of the past five thousand years. In the Christian story, the scapegoating culminates in Jesus himself, who becomes the divine rescuer who alone can guarantee redemption and salvation. But wanton violence continues throughout the whole of creation, and apparently will continue while patriarchy prevails.

It is not humans nor the living earth that is flawed, but patriarchy itself. A growing body of adult people of faith are beginning to suspect where the real truth lies, leading already to extensive critiques of redemptive violence (Ruether 1998; Ray 1998; Patterson 2004; Brock and Parker 2008), and will lead to even more radical evaluation as we move deeper into the twenty-first century.

3. Obey the Rules

Redemption/salvation demands of passive humans allegiance to conditions, prescriptions, and regulations. Whether intentionally or not, formal religion tends to convey a sense of universal human unworthiness, in the face of which God must be compensated, pacified, and honored in some superhuman exalted fashion. Conditions abound. "Shoulds," "ifs," "buts," and "musts" dominate the religious vocabulary. It is hard to avoid the conclusion that this is a divine projection with features of the patriarchal demanding father-figure who requires absolute submission from those expected to remain permanently in a state of childlike dependence and obedience.

This demanding type of religiosity still holds some appeal for peoples living in extreme poverty and oppressive conditions. Striving to be faithful to this demanding father God gives the semblance of feeling good about oneself, knowing that one is "succeeding" in being religiously faithful. Consequently, one hopes that God will hear and respond, and even if "He" does not, at least he will be lenient on the day of judgment. Even among the poor and marginalized, this distorted spirituality is wearing thin. Many contemporary adults, brought up in this punitive type of religion, have long ago outgrown it.

4. The Violent Conquest

The domination and control, exercised in the name of the divine ruling God, is saturated in the dynamics of violence, sometimes overtly in the God who kills and destroys (and favors humans who do likewise), or covertly in the hidden wounds of fear, guilt and unworthiness, pervasively known and experienced in various religious cultures. Walter Wink (1992, 33) captures this disturbing deviation when he writes:

> How did the Domination System get started? The myth of redemptive violence gives this answer: war, conquest, plunder, rape, and enslavement are all ordained in the very constitution of the universe, which itself is formed from the corpse of a murdered goddess. "Civilization" is a condition of periodic or perpetual warfare, "peace" the achievement of warfare, "prosperity" the fruit of warfare successfully accomplished. If human beings are created from the blood of a slaughtered God, how can one expect from them anything but violence?

Beyond Dysfunctional Religion

Humans are blessed with an innate sense of what is right and wrong, of what is authentic and false. In a range of paradoxical ways we honor this intuitive wisdom. In times of cultural breakdown we exhibit contradictory behaviors, yet the will-to-meaning wins out in the long term. We need an evolutionary, long-term context to see the truth of these otherwise contradictory claims.

Today, humans are beginning to address the inherited dysfunctionality of religion. This will be a long process and, as already intimated, not without contradiction. People of more adult insight and wisdom are beginning to grasp the inherited dysfunctionality of formal religion, registering their disagreement, and in a range of different ways distancing themselves from what they perceive to be no longer life-giving.

Various reformers have attempted to revitalize their religious systems, with limited success. In an attempt to become more relevant, religions try to present a friendlier face; make more extensive use of mass media; dialogue more extensively with their followers; make worship more attractive; improve their social image, especially in concern for justice (personal and ecological); be more inclusive of women and social minorities. However, the basic structural model, prioritizing patriarchal governance, has remained largely unchanged. Clergy may consult people a great deal more, and even create structures for mutual accountability, but nobody is in any doubt on who has the final word and who is ultimately in control.

The insidious power of the patriarchal base is particularly noticeable in the Catholic Church. The Catholic populace on the one hand and the media on the other tend to judge the entire organization in terms of Rome, and the hierarchy representing the Roman power. One notes in conversations among Catholics how quickly the focus of attention consistently veers toward the clergy, the bishops, Rome! Similarly, in the popular press attention is rarely given to what ordinary Catholics do at the base of the organization, where millions live out their faith with great generosity of spirit, courageous witness, and frequently with little concern for what Rome says or does. Here we encounter a serious dilemma with a significant impact on the appropriation of adult faith.

Currently, the Catholic Church consists of 1.2 billion people, of which fewer than 500,000 members make up the hierarchical dimension, consisting of ordained deacons, priests, bishops, cardinals, and the pope. In other words the hierarchical dimension makes up less than *one-tenth of 1 percent,* a tiny fraction of the entire body. Why then is everybody, media included, so preoccupied with Rome and the concerns of the hierarchy? Why is not more attention given to the body — the nonclericalized domain — where millions live out their faith each day?

Here we confront a dysfunctionality of grave proportions. A lurid fascination prevails regarding the tiny sector, onto which all the power is projected. Of course those at the top want it that way, but why do the people continue to collude with it? The average Catholic is likely to respond that the imbalance is a product of history about which the people can do little or nothing — change has to come from the top down. Historically change rarely comes from the top down.

Ironically, the preoccupation with hierarchical power in Roman Catholicism may be first and foremost a people's problem, and it may be largely in the hands of the people to resolve it. Past conditioning has been so strong, people cannot even think "adult": come to the awareness that the problem with power is actually being fed and sustained by the people's own acquiescence and collusion. Even those who heavily criticize church power and authority may be nourishing the dysfunctionality by their criticizing; the criticism itself — especially when abetted by the media — is like a supply of energy helping to maintain the existence of the dysfunctional behavior.

What needs to happen for a religion like Roman Catholicism is for the people to withdraw their projections and give their energy instead to creative alternatives. This is broadly what began to happen to parts of Latin America with the rise of basic Christian communities in the 1970s and 1980s. Rome reacted — because it felt so threatened. Sociologically, this is exactly what we would have expected. Some commentators claim that the BCC movement has been crushed entirely. I suspect it has been driven underground and is being maintained by those who seek to honor the *adult* in their faith development. Meanwhile, millions in Latin America have drifted away from Catholicism; Rome's heavy-handedness backfired, and the disempowered chose other ways to retain their sense of personal power.

Many commentators have highlighted the abusive nature of religious power and domination, but few have highlighted the contribution that people themselves make by maintaining — unawares — the abusive system. Only when enough people reclaim their *adult* selves, read the reality with greater depth and wisdom, learn to withdraw (or withhold) the collusions and projections, then the patriarchal system can be starved of energy and will eventually collapse. And all the religious rhetoric on earth will not be able to keep it alive.

This does not mean abandoning or betraying the church. It may not even involve leaving the church. It evokes and invites a whole different sense of what it means to be a religious believer and what it means to be a participant in a credible faith community. It translates into making a choice not to compromise the call to be *adult* in how one engages growth in faith — one's own and that of others. I will return to this challenge in Part Two.

*(a) **Conventional inherited** wisdom uses guilt and fear to maintain fidelity (that is, submissiveness) to the patriarchal controlling God, whose will for humanity is best accessed through a literal interpretation of Holy Writ and those who legislate on the basis of such an appropriation of sacred scripture.*

*(b) **Embedded codependency** seeks to keep people feeling fearful and unworthy so that control can be exerted as strongly as possible.*

*(c) **Adult empowerment** begins with releasing something of what constricts and binds. Millions have already done this in a kind of reckless abandonment. And by opting for a more covenantal, convivial understanding of the mystery within which we — and all creation — are held, then we can become the beneficiaries of divine empowerment.*

Chapter Four

The Tyranny of the Rational Mind

FOCUS: If you can defend your position using logical, rational argument, you stand a much better chance of being treated like an adult. According to this expectation, emotion, feeling, intuition, and imagination are held suspect. Genuine adulthood cannot be realized without the incorporation of all aspects.

> *Many of us reach adulthood with our exuberance not only tamed but domesticated. Our well socialized selves distrust spontaneity. Our stance toward life is responsible, resigned, or resentful, but enthusiasm is rare. We feel stuck, embedded in duties yet somehow disconnected from life. Eros seems to have retreated, taking with it vitality and joy.*
>
> — JAMES AND EVELYN WHITEHEAD

I N AN OFT CITED ARTICLE, Arlene W. Saxonhouse (1988) reminds us that the early Greeks invoked the notion of reason almost as a new form of tyranny. Their goal was to counteract the tyranny of the irrational mind whereby humans were perceived to be overattached to the physical world. Authentic humanity could evolve only separated from and over against the natural environment that for far too long kept humans trapped in what the Greeks perceived to be the tyranny of nature itself. Humans, being the supreme species (according to classical Greek thought) should differentiate and separate by adopting the power of rational reason (also de Sousa 2007; Ralston Saul 1994).

Humans, it was argued, were endowed with "higher" capabilities, requiring them to differentiate from nature, and through the power of that which made them different — namely, the capacity for rational choice — they should take control of the world, molding and fashioning it to their own ends and purposes.

The Fallacy of Rationality

The Australian ecofeminist Val Plumwood offers a penetrating and informed analysis of our inherited Greek tradition, with its heavy emphasis on rationality, dualism, disconnection from the earth, and the compulsion for masculine domination and control. She writes: "This reason-centered culture has become a liability to survival. Reason has been made a vehicle for domination and death. We must change this culture or face extinction" (Plumwood 2002, 5).

The system is little more than twenty-five hundred years old, and therefore unknown to the human species for millions of years previously. Rational perception and discourse actually flourishes on a preposterous sense of blindness: namely, that our human existence prior to about five thousand years ago was totally enmeshed with the natural world: primitive, prelogical, and basically inhuman. For the new "liberators," humans had to be extricated from this barbaric codependence so that they could enter the free, differentiated world of Greek metaphysics with its heavy emphasis on cerebral logic and the use of reason.

The plot is thick with contradictions, riddled with projections, and infiltrated with a plethora of unexamined assumptions. Today the growing body of anthropological and palaeontological research exposes the fallacies of the Aristotelian worldview. Correcting the view is one major task; more formidable and disturbing for the powers that be is the liberating empowerment that ensues. When too many people begin to reclaim what they never should have been denied, namely, the right to live their lives as useful, fulfilled adult beings, then those in charge begin to feel threatened.

And the controlling logic also becomes quite scared of the new integration. Feeling, intuition, imagination, and emotion begin to reclaim their legitimate place in the grand scheme of human flourishing. The multidimensional aspects of human nature are acknowledged and legitimized — at least in theory. The authentic adult human now stands a better chance of evolving out of the dark and oppressive shadows of the Greek metaphysical worldview.

Val Plumwood spells out some of the subtle dynamics of Western rationality in what she describes as "a systemic pattern of distortions and illusions" (Plumwood 2002, 16). These need to be named before we can hope to transcend their disabling power. Some elements will need to be abandoned; they have served their time and purpose. Others can be transformed so that they can be reused to serve the more holistic and adult worldview emerging in our time.

To the fore is the distortion that requires all rational humans to be *impartial to alterity,* the need to retain an emotional distance from the otherness of the earth, which is merely an object perceived to be alien to our human subjectivity. On the human level, the otherness to be overcome came to be identified with the power of the feminine, embodied primarily in the woman. The sphere of private emotion was projected onto all that represented the feminine, deemed to be inferior to the power of public reason, associated primarily with dominant males.

A second major distortion gives rise to *dualisms* and the felt need to split everything in life into pairs of binary opposites: earth v. heaven; body v. soul; matter v. spirit. All dualisms are inventions of the rational human mind. Throughout creation, mutual interdependence is the governing principle, employing a polarity of both-and not a dualism of either-or. In a word, all dualisms are false and despite their practical usefulness will never lead to wholesome outcomes.

The third distortion is based on the assumption that has come to be known as *the fundamental flaw,* which translates into the religious notion of *original sin.* It is based on a rather primitive underlying assumption, that human nature is essentially corrupt, due to a rebellion that took place in heaven many aeons ago. Consequently — and this is the outrageous anthropocentric projection — all life, including the earth and the cosmos, is fundamentally flawed.

The fourth and final distortion postulates *a ruling male God requiring on earth male representatives* who can rule, govern, and control in a rational way. Steve Taylor (2005) describes this development as *the ego explosion*. Historically and geographically he locates the shift toward distorted rationality within the emergence of the agricultural revolution, enabling us to see that the disempowerment of adult people is closely connected to the disempowerment of the earth itself. Ironically, that same disregard for the living earth is a major obstacle to the realization of authentic adulthood in our time as well.

Rationality and the Evolution of Agriculture

The agricultural revolution tends to be dated to about ten thousand years ago and lasted for several subsequent millennia. It marks a new sense of engagement with the productive potential of the land, projecting humans — males particularly — into an aggressive, manipulative, divisive, and violent relationship toward the use of land. It marks the violent departure from the hunter-gatherer way of life in which nature provided for everybody, shifting instead to the culture of mass production and the consequent objectification of the land. The latter benefits primarily those who owned and controlled the use of the land, those with a quality of power that disempowered most others and prevented them from becoming adults in their own right.[3]

Some commentators naively assume that the development of agriculture in this period reaped widespread benefits for the human population of the time. To the contrary, it seems to have had quite deleterious effects on the health of the majority of people. Stringer and McKie (1996, 222) make the interesting observation that when maize was introduced into the diet of American Indians in the Midwest, about a thousand years ago, the general state of health deteriorated quite suddenly. Tooth cavities jumped sevenfold; anemia quadrupled in frequency; tuberculosis, yaws, osteo-arthritis, and syphilis were noted in large numbers of a previously healthy population. Pregnant mothers were known to be particularly undernourished, and about a fifth of the population died in infancy.

The agricultural revolution initiated a profound shift in human consciousness, the nature of which still defies human comprehension.

Steve Taylor (2005) offers one of the more informed analyses, focusing particularly on the destruction of the rich fertile plains of North Africa and the sudden emergence of desert conditions in a region that he names "Saharasia." In humans, a new psychic shift took place, characterized by separation from nature, new levels of insecurity and anxiety, and a shift in personal power that he designates "the ego explosion." He describes the process in these words:

> The Ego Explosion was the most momentous event in the history of the human race. The last 6,000 years of history can only be understood in terms of it. All of the different kinds of social and psychic pathology — war, patriarchy, social stratification, materialism, the desire for status and power, sexual repression, environmental destruction, as well as inner discontent and disharmony which afflict us — all of these traits can be traced back to the intensified sense of ego which came into existence in the deserts of Saharasia 6,000 years ago. (Taylor 2005, 124)

The patriarchal system as we know it today came into being (possibly for the first time). A new caste came to the fore, predominantly male, with an intense desire for domination and control, using excessive rationality. Their primary target was the human being deranged by the fundamental flaw, yet potentially capable of being restored to full rationality — thus entitled to rule over human life and over all other life forms as well. The way to do it was to develop a structure similar to what they thought prevailed in heaven: a powerful male deity totally in control of everything beneath him and delegating his authority downward to the select few who, on behalf of the ruling God, would dominate and control everybody else.

In this scheme, only God, and those designated to act on God's behalf, are deemed to be adult — and rational. Everybody else is a passive, codependent, subservient creature. Men are primarily in charge, since they alone can use reason in a truly responsible way. And since women are prone to hysteria, they need to be kept in their subservient place.

Control from a Distance

Rationality relies heavily on the power of words, argumentation, and monolithic persuasion. Only one truth is tolerated and that belongs to the few who hold the power. To implement the disempowering strategy, boundaries and barriers are firmly set in place and fiercely guarded. A systemic distancing reinforces the will to power and domination. This is what Plumwood (2002) calls "systemic remoteness," originally named by Dryzek (1987). Val Plumwood (2002, 72) identifies five articulations:

1. *spatial remoteness:* maintaining an experiential distance from the situation about which one is making a decision, in which case one has no personal understanding of the direct adversarial effects;

2. *consequential remoteness:* some other person or group is blamed for consequences arising from the behavior of the third party;

3. *communicative/epistemic remoteness:* blocked communication, weakening the real truth of a situation, e.g., Roman authorities condemning theologians without ever communicating with them as persons;

4. *temporal remoteness:* refusing to consider the long-term consequences of a decision or an action;

5. *technological remoteness:* using technology for personal or localized comfort, failing to attend to the deleterious effects on the wider environment.

Not only do these strategies reinforce the will to power, to the benefit of the few; they also effectively neutralize any possibility for collaborative power-sharing. And this is where so-called democratic governments fail dismally in calling forth the adult amid the human masses. Codependency and disempowerment reign supreme, even in advanced nations. And millions are left disenfranchised and disillusioned.

A dangerous psychosocial deviancy also ensues, named by the American moral theologian Mark Jordan (2000) as "the rhetoric of tedium." Those embedded in the rationalistic way of being can be overwhelming in their use of words and the impressive logic of their arguments. But they often leave listeners cold, untouched and even bored. The rhetoric is impressive and subtly if not overtly aimed at control. It does not touch the heart and frequently is not coming from the heart either. In our world of mass information, such rhetoric alienates people, often engendering cynicism and, in extreme cases, violent reaction.

Robust Individualism

The cult of cynicism begets a range of cultural responses that baffle and confuse many people today and, as we might expect, tend to be harshly judged by the guardians of orthodoxy. These cultural responses have been labeled as the cult of *postmodernism*. Millions take life into their own hands, do things their own way, prioritize their own development and seem not to care much about universally shared values or what is sometimes called the common good. Selfishness, greed, and the cult of the self seem to dominate our contemporary landscape, accompanied by a widespread disregard for public polity and the social fabric of civilization.

The phenomenon has been extensively studied, but in most cases from within the Western academic world. The analysis highlights a central predicament but offers little toward understanding or resolution. I wish to suggest that the culture of postmodernism is for the greater part a cultural reaction to the extreme rationalism of the dominant culture itself. In a word, millions are fed up with being disenfranchised, controlled, dominated, and grossly disempowered. They see no rational way of reclaiming their personal and adult integrity. So they opt for the irrational and set out to reclaim — often recklessly — all that has been robbed from them.

The new individualism is not some postmodernist reckless option, but in fact a direct consequence of the cult of rationality, which I have briefly critiqued above. Those who never made it, those who never could — and there are millions of them — are the ones left with such deep levels of psychic emptiness that they cannot but resort to compensatory tactics. What is at work here is the innate wisdom of the subconscious psyche. As typically happens in the cult of rationality, we judge the symptoms, the external behaviors, and we often miss the subtle undercurrents, the search for meaning coming from deep within.

We can identify three stages that characterize growth into authentic adulthood: *dependence, independence,* and *interdependence.* These could be renamed as "me-only," "me-over-against-others," and "me-with-others." Human life begins in a state of total dependence on the other, primarily on the nurturing mother. Throughout our early formative years we are dependent on parents, guardians, teachers, and many others. During adolescence, we move into a phase of independence, initially reactionary, and gradually moving toward a more proactive stance. This movement from dependence to independence is essential if we are to function healthily in the world.

It is, however, quite a complex transition. The developmental stage of adolescence has become quite open-ended. Some theorists like Robert Epstein (2007) argue that the concept of adolescence is essentially flawed, the creation of a culture unable to move meaningfully from childhood into adulthood. Most development psychologists would disagree, seeing it as a necessary stage and one that today no longer ends in our late teens but may be prolonged well into our twenties, or even into our early thirties. It is also well known that some reawakenings during the midlife stage (anywhere from thirty-five to fifty-five) reenact adolescent rebellion; regression to teenage moods, fantasies, and reactions can easily become part of one's behavioral repertoire.

Ideally, a third stage, namely, *interdependence,* should, and usually does, emerge, but for many this does not happen in the twenties or thirties, as is generally assumed, but in the post-midlife phase — usually after the age of fifty. In Jungian psychology it is named as a process of *individuation,* an evolving awareness of my interconnectedness, not just with other people, but with every organism that constitutes the web of life. This is the context in which adulthood stands the best chance of being more fully realized.

A New Kind of Heroism

In classical antiquity, and in ancient Greek religion, veneration of deified heroes such as Heracles, Perseus, and Achilles played an important role. Heroes in myth often had close but conflicted relationships with the gods. This sense of divine power, accompanied by magic and superhuman endowments, is the basis of various popular myths, ancient and modern.

The metaphor of the hero is endemic to patriarchal cultures. It depicts the dominant male (only on rare occasions have females been truly heroic), of impressive presence, controlling the entire plot and aiming at maximum achievement. Self-sacrifice is inherent to this undertaking, but more significantly, the sacrifice of many others (human and nonhuman), is the price to be paid for the hero to realize his full potential.

The hero indulges in battle; in fact, he seems to be in a permanent state of conflict with "the forces of evil." The late Michael Jackson, iconic pop hero who died in June 2009, embodied numerous features of the mythic hero and subconsciously was "worshiped" by millions around the world. What many failed to realize is that Jackson also embodied the deconstruction of the archetype of the hero, a cultural process that has been evolving since the early 1960s.

As a cultural icon the myth of the hero began to crumble in the 1960s. This was especially noticeable in the United States as the veterans came back from Vietnam, and many did not acclaim them as heroes. In fact, they were widely regarded as foolish for having gone there in the first place. The focus for being a hero began to shift from public patriarchal figures of the military, the government, and the church to heroic idols in music, sport, and, to a lesser extent, the arts.

The collapse of the archetypal hero into a range of more narcissistic, hedonistic, playful, *irrational* articulations was widely derided and condemned as another postmodern deviation. But few understood the cultural and archetypal significance of what was transpiring. Paradoxically, it was a process of rehabilitation rather than betrayal, and a few insightful visionaries glimpsed the radical nature of what was unfolding.

The American philosopher Sam Keen (1985) captivates quite profoundly the shift I am describing. He claims that our modern civilization is not merely challenging the metaphor of the hero. It has already displaced that icon of the hero and replaced it with a new explosive metaphor, namely, that of the *lover*. No more heroes. Let's get rid of them and replace them with lovers. The implications of this new iconic image will be explored in Part Two of this book.

Reclaiming the Vulnerable Adult

What Aristotle described as the tyranny of the irrational has come back to haunt the human species. The tyranny of rationality is imploding — on a global scale. Herbert Marcuse's one-dimensional man is becoming multidimensional, the protean human whose capacity for rational reason is supplemented by, and often subjected to, other dimensions of human experience, such as the social, the emotional, the intellectual, the spiritual and the psychic. The very essence of what it means to be human is being renegotiated and redefined. In this new cultural context, the adult as adult stands a much better chance of flourishing anew.

Perhaps the single greatest challenge in this transformative process is the need to reclaim the vulnerable adult. This in fact is the inner self we have known over millions of years of our earlier evolution as a human species. Vulnerability is a graced gift. It keeps us close to the tenderness and fragility of all living organisms. It keeps us more open and receptive to the surprise of the new. And it alerts us to the dangerous allurement of heroic power games.

The prevailing world order cannot tolerate weakness, vulnerability, and those levels of pain and suffering that are endemic to our evolutionary unfolding. Evolutionary emergence triumphs on the recurring cycle of birth–death–rebirth. The pain of letting go, the ability to befriend diminishment, the wisdom to die to that which is no longer useful are all inherent dimensions of our paradoxical creation and foundational to the "progress" of evolution itself. To many it does not make rational sense — many features of evolutionary growth and development do not make rational sense. Rather, it embraces a wisdom that transcends the narrow and suffocating imperialism of excessive rationalism.

Science desperately wants to get rid of all suffering in human life. Religion tends to explain it away, but suffering because of our sins, or to procure credit in a life hereafter, command little credibility in the modern world. Culturally and spiritually, we have lost the ancient wisdom that can integrate suffering into the larger scheme of evolutionary change and growth. And this integration makes us more compassionate people, more tolerant, more caring, and thus more empowering in calling forth the best in each other, for adult and child alike.

When Heroes Give Way to Lovers

As I conclude this section, I want to illustrate the subtle and pervasive nature of Sam Keen's suggestive shift in contemporary cultural metaphors. The first Gulf war (1990–91) evoked numerous peace protests around the world. In one mass rally in London, the gay-lesbian community carried a large float that caught the attention of media around the world. The banner read: "Take our men to bed, not to war!" A poignant and powerful statement of the shift from the metaphor of the hero to that of the lover!

In the contemporary world, the metaphor of the lover dominates the landscape. Paradoxically our world needs the energy of true love more than anything else at this time of so much violence, warfare, and social disintegration. Metaphors often operate in this strangely paradoxical way. The new metaphor, like many novel ideas, initially evokes a negative reaction, a defensive response arising from fear and threat. It is almost as if the guardians of the old know that the new will eventually assume a leading role.

As a cultural catalyst, the metaphor of the lover came to the fore in the 1960s. Free love became a new and disruptively dangerous idea. Ethical and cultural boundaries were transgressed, sometimes with a rapidity that defied credibility and a brashness that showed little respect for traditional wisdom. Young people explored other nations and cultures; religions entered into new alliances; spiritual practices such as meditation attracted people from divergent backgrounds. But most alarming of all was the psychosexual transition. Conventional sexual norms were thrown overboard. Genital sexual behavior abandoned the exclusive enclave of heterosexual monogamous marriage and became a dimension of various new liaisons. Sex for procreation gave way to sex for recreation. To some, it felt as if all hell had broken lose.

Out of this dangerously paradoxical milieu emerged the new adult being described in the pages of this book. It was anything but an idyllic virgin birth. It had chaos written all over it, and still has. This is how major evolutionary shifts tend to happen. The prevailing rational wisdom responded in the only way it could, the only way it knew, with rejection and denunciation.

Fortunately, evolution does not wait for human planners, nor for the approval of our conventional institutions. It follows a deeper suprarational wisdom and seeks out other types of heroes to pick up the baton. These become the reckless lovers that carry us over the new evolutionary threshold. Their identity and mission become clearer in Part Two of this book.

(a) *Conventional inherited wisdom prioritizes those skilled in deductive, controlling reason. They become the heroes to which everybody else must subject themselves; we learn to imitate them as the true and reliable guides of enduring values.*

(b) *Embedded codependence assumes that most people (and the earth itself) are passive and not very intelligent. The divine inherited wisdom is invested in the select few, whose heroic skill at rational wisdom will bring salvation to all the others.*

(c) *Adult empowerment cherishes lovers rather than heroes. It celebrates a diversity of gifts and talents to be used for the mutual benefit of all and for the benefit of the living earth, where no one set of creatures is rated higher or more significant than others.*

Chapter Five

Our Frazzled Institutions

FOCUS: All the major institutions we know today evolved as instruments for the implementation of patriarchal power. Many are breaking down and losing credibility, giving way to networks with a greater potential for collaboration and adult empowerment.

The ultimate metaphysical principle is the advance from dysfunction to conjunction, creating a novel entity other than the entities given in disjunction.   — A. N. WHITEHEAD

I T DID NOT HAPPEN immediately after 9/11, the violent collapse of the twin towers in New York in September 2001. It started to unravel about five years later. The U.S. dollar began to lose its value against other international currencies. Within the United States itself, consumerism moved into overdrive, with banks recklessly lending money to insatiable speculators and property tycoons. Meanwhile, millions of dollars were being poured into Iraq and Afghanistan on an annual basis. Life went on as if all was well. It was anything but well, with a deadly cancer eating its way into the U.S. economy — and lethal consequences for every nation on earth were to follow.

Finally, in 2008 the United States woke up. The major financial institutions were in disarray. Thousands were losing their jobs. Banks had to be bailed out — all because of reckless banking speculators who gambled millions with little or no accountability. Strangely, most of them were granted "immunity," although some did resign. By then the crisis had reached Europe, Japan, India, and even China. Something suspiciously fragile seemed to characterize the resilient "unregulated" market.

People of deeper vision spoke their truth to power, but as one might expect those in power chose not to listen. The visionaries spoke of the end of capitalism, or at least the beginning of the end. Who would dare entertain such a frightening prospect! The impervious divine market might be enduring a crisis, but most considered it just a passing blip that could be rectified by more reckless borrowing (ironically, the strategy adopted by Gordon Brown in the UK and by Barack Obama in the United States). At any cost, capitalism has to be kept alive — even if it is dying on its feet.

How right Walter Brueggemann (1986, 26) was when he wrote:

A frightened, crushed imagination has been robbed of power precisely because of fear. Indeed, one can note the abysmal lack of imagination in the formation of policy about either international security or domestic economics. We can think of nothing to do except do more of the same, which generates only more problems and more fear.

The Institutional Death Knell

The financial crisis of the early twenty-first century serves as a useful example of the institutional collapse that is extensive in the modern world but largely unrecognized because of petrified denial. The nation-state itself struggles to retain credibility (Laitin 2007; Ohmae 2005; *http://libertariannation.org/b/demise.htm*). Even the mighty empire of the United States asked for international support in trying to rectify or reverse the financial crisis of 2008. Banking institutions are more vulnerable than anybody had suspected. Education, health care and social systems all show signs of vulnerability, while churches and religions, preoccupied with self-preservation, have little or nothing to offer to the confused and frightened masses at this time.

All major institutions are in a state of identity crisis. What are they about? What purpose do they serve? Have they a future? People of adult integrity ask such questions and expect honest answers. These are the questions that should guide our discernment, but most people are too scared to entertain such a fundamental analysis.

Our cultural conditioning also creates serious barriers. The suggested collapse of capitalism can only mean one thing for most people: the revival of socialism. We don't seem to have the imaginative versatility to dream other alternatives. Nor indeed are we capable of discerning what exactly we mean by "socialism" in terms of alternatives that have been tried, some successfully, others less so. A great deal of ideological clutter gets in the way, particularly the confusion between socialism and Marxism, or worse still the identification of Marxism with communism.

Once again, power raises its ugly head. Socialism, no matter how we define it, involves a sharing of power. Less opportunity for the fierce competitor, but more potential for cooperation and mutual enhancement, values cherished by people of more adult stature. Too much to lose for those who like to do business as usual, and monopolize for themselves as much as possible, but not much to gain for the millions subdued for too long to the plight of powerlessness and often abject poverty.

Thus far nobody points the finger at the nation-state itself! According to all three monotheistic religions (Christianity, Judaism, and Islam) the nation-state is God's divinely decreed way for governance on this earth. In other words, God has chosen the nation-state above any other political entity. This religious rationale is much more pervasive than we think and has contributed significantly to many of the major wars and international conflicts of the twentieth century.

We need to wake up and face the fact that the nation-state is a human invention and certainly not a stroke of genius arising either from ingenuity or human intelligence. It is the strategy devised to govern and control an unruly earth belonging to an unruly people. The carving up of the planet has been done in a capricious, thoughtless, brutal fashion. The colonial aftermath of the eighteenth and nineteenth centuries still haunts many African countries striving to develop empowering structures to foster progress and prosperity. No wonder wars have been fought — and I suspect always will be while we refuse to reassess the dysfunctional aftermath of our imperial will to power.

As global markets came to the fore in the closing decades of the twentieth century, nation-states lost a great deal of political and financial clout. Trade was dictated by anonymous market forces; prices were leveled by other international agencies, e.g., the WTO (World Trade Organization). Access to goods and services was controlled by major corporations; even patents on various resources were held by corporations and not by nation-states (after 1994). Globalization robbed the nation-states of control, despite the fact that it is the nations themselves that agreed to this (by submitting to WTO regulation).

Despite attempts to reclaim lost national power in the opening decade of the twenty-first century, the concept of the nation-state is still a very precarious one with two alternative forces cocreating a different future: *globalization* and *international networking*. The energy-for-networking is particularly significant, and ever since the conception of the NGO in the 1940s, world governance through the nation-state has receded in favor of governance through networking facilities. Although not formally acknowledged anywhere on earth, I suspect this movement toward *the priority of networks* is much further advanced than we care to acknowledge. In all probability it will emerge as the leading political configuration for the twenty-first century.

Institutions Disempower

Modern institutions are the progeny of the patriarchal will to power and evolved as mechanisms to exercise domination and absolute control. And those called to control assumed they were divinely mandated to do so. Power belonged to those called forth to govern. Historically that has been done by the ruling king, and in some cultures of the past five thousand years, the king was deemed to be divine, or at least semi-divine. In the Hebrew scriptures, God's primary representative on earth is not the priest, but the king. And the king's palace, not the temple, is deemed to be the primary abode of God on earth.

In this model, adulthood pertains primarily to those who govern. And throughout the patriarchal era (approximately the past ten thousand years), only males were deemed suitable for governance. This means that women were barred from any recognition of being adult in their own right. Consequently, until the late 1800s women were not allowed to vote in most countries.

Adulthood, therefore, is synonymous with power, and power is primarily a male prerogative. Empowerment has no place in this dispensation. All power is held by God, who chooses to dispense of it through chosen males on earth. It is to be exercised over (not shared with) all inferior creatures, humans and nonhumans alike. Humans had to devise whatever structures are necessary to exercise this power-over. They chose institutional structures with a clear-cut chain of command from top to bottom and frequently enforced their authority through brutality and violence. Ironically the more passive they made the people, the more the people revolted and the harder it was to exercise absolute control.

Institutions inherently disempower. Those at the base of the hierarchy, which will always be the majority, resent being trodden upon, even when it is done in a benign fashion, even when great wealth and progress ensues. Every democratic country invests enormous sums of money to keep social deviancy at bay. Policing the "powerful" system against the threat of "terrorism" now costs the human community billions of dollars, while millions of people are so disempowered culturally and psychologically they could scarcely muster the energy to commit a deviant act. One begins to wonder who feeds the terrorism of which the West particularly is so scared.

No matter how democratic a hierarchical system is, it will fail to do justice to the aspirations of the people. People want to participate; they want to be involved; in a word, they want to exercise their adult creativity. And when that goal is jeopardized, it is then we need policing, legal systems that tend to be very expensive, resorting to imprisonment and incarcerations. The prevailing power — culturally, politically, and religiously — feeds power. Only in a minimal and superficial way does it empower.

Networking: The Way Forward

To offset the negative impact of the Great Depression in the 1930s and the threat to global harmony posed by the Second World War, the United Nations came into being on October 24, 1945. Its dangerous, prophetic vision was quickly domesticated and curtailed, and for much of its existence its capacity for empowerment has been seriously hampered by the superpowers of the former Soviet Union and the U.S. government. Its internal procedures prioritize the nation-state, and this has seriously jeopardized its potential to serve as an international global voice for all earth's people and resources, as stated in the Earth Charter, formalized on June 29, 2000.

The cultural and prophetic impact of the UN has rarely been acknowledged; indeed, it would be both subversive and dangerous to do so. At the heart of the dream that gave birth to the UN is the cultural aspiration of *one people inhabiting one earth*. The envisaged unity of the human species within cultural diversity and the essential unity of the earth itself are key elements in this new global village. Behind the external explanations and legal details is a cultural and spiritual invitation to become once more a unified species on the one earth. The nation-state is called to serve this ideal, and not be merely the primary mechanism through which the dream is mediated.

Despite the official rhetoric prioritizing the nation-state, the subconscious dream behind the vision of the UN is to supersede the nation-state and replace it with a form of governance that would honor the aspiration of one people inhabiting one earth. That underlying subversive vision broke through in 1945 when the UN gave birth to the concept of the NGO (nongovernmental organization). In a desire to empower the disempowered masses, the NGO was to function as a facilitating organism between people and formal government, whereby people could get more ready access to governmental resources, and governments could become more responsive to the people's real needs.

The concept of the NGO has had quite a checkered history. At the end of the day it was up to national governments to adopt or reject the concept. Even where the UN itself tried to work primarily through NGOs, especially in the Southern Hemisphere, not all governments cooperated, and when they did cooperate, they quickly reacted to the power — and threat — of this new movement. They effectively domesticated NGOs into government agencies, thus stripping them of their empowering potential.

Meanwhile, the NGO veered off in another direction, in what initially seemed to be innocuous to mainline governments and posing no threat to their power. The concept of the NGO came to be identified with the wider trend of *networking,* fluid and flexible ways of organizing, largely devoid of patriarchal manipulation and control and aimed primarily at empowering people from the base up. Basic Christian communities (BCCs) became the religious expression of this same development.

Organizationally, networking is an illusive concept but culturally enjoys widespread recognition. Paul Hawken (2007) is among the better known contemporary proponents, and his prophetic and hope-filled insights will be reviewed in Part Two of this book.

The Subversive Power of Cooperation

Competition is a core value of capitalism and of modern economic globalization. From a very young age our children are brainwashed into becoming fierce competitors. Some theorists consider this to be an inherited trait of our evolutionary history, evidenced in the behavior of certain animals and primates.

Not all specialists agree. The self-fulfilling prophesy of our normative patriarchal culture has been subjected to some serious critique in recent decades. To the fore is the pioneering work of microbiologist Lynn Margulis (1998), whose theory of *symbiogenesis* offers a challenging counterview. Having devoted a lifetime to the study of bacterial organic life, Margulis highlights an unmistakable orientation, not for competition but for *cooperation.* Her controversial insights have been endorsed by scholars such as Frans de Waal (2005), Jane Goodall (2001), and Sarah Blaffer Hrdy (2009).

Claiming cooperation to be distinctively unique for humans, Sarah Blaffer Hrdy (2009) sees the parental dependency of early childhood as unambiguous evidence for cooperative imprinting. She writes (Hrdy, 6–7):

> Humans are born predisposed to care how they relate to others. A growing body of research is persuading neuroscientists that Baruch Spinoza's seventeenth-century proposal better captures the full range of tensions humans grow up with. "The endeavor to live in a shared, peaceful agreement with others is an extension of the endeavor to preserve oneself." Emerging evidence is drawing psychologists and economists alike to conclude that "our brains are wired to cooperate with others" as well as to reward or punish others for mutual cooperation. . . . New discoveries of evolutionarily minded psychologists, economists, and neuroscientists are propelling the cooperative side of human nature to center stage.

Human imagination has been domesticated within a number of key institutions that impinge upon our daily lives, mainly through culture and governance. These include the family unit (nuclear and extended), schools, hospitals, business organizations, public media, formal religions, and various layers of government bureaucracy. In most of these institutions the human being is seen primarily as a deviant creature whose behavior has to be tightly controlled. Instead of being perceived as creative adults, whose long evolutionary history verifies — with increasing scientific affirmation — a heavy commitment to conviviality and collaboration (see O'Murchu 2008), humans have been subjected to highly destructive imperial control. And we wonder why our way of being in the world has become so violent and destructive!

The major institutions we have cocreated served us through a problematic evolutionary period in which male dominance prevailed (the postagricultural phase). It has not always been like that, and it certainly must change if humanity wishes to enjoy a new and more fruitful phase of growth and development. In this chapter I have highlighted some of the changing orientations in our structural ways of being in the world, the adopting of social and political alternatives congenial to more integrated, creative, and dynamic ways of living. How these are likely to evolve in the future is explored in Part Two.

Fluid Structures

Any critique of our dominant institutions will tend to evoke a defensive reaction. Those with vested interests, and the many people who have been coopted, fear that anarchy might break loose if the grip of control is loosened in any way. Deviancy, and not creativity, is seen as the core driving force in the human will-to-meaning. It is at this juncture that adult integrity is compromised to a degree that oppresses millions all over the world and ironically leads to more and not less deviant behavior.

In the above critique of patriarchally inspired systems, the suggested devolution of major institutions should not be seen as an automatic prescription for anarchy and a reckless free-for-all. We are social creatures and will always need social structures to function creatively in the world. The distinction between *institutions* and *structures* is crucial to this analysis. Institutions denote a top-down hierarchical line of control, usually with clear distinctions between "us" (at the top) and "them" (at the base). Such an arrangement is culturally and historically time-conditioned. There are other structural strategies that can be employed, far more liberating and empowering and far more conducive to embracing and advancing the creative adult of our time.

As already indicated, the *network* seems to be the favored alternative for the future. Characterized by fluidity and flexibility, it is much more capable of honoring human creativity for the benefit of person and planet alike. As a local endeavor the concept of networking is already well established. It is the networking of the networks that is still very new, and not easily conceptualized in terms of national or international governance. Potentially, the United Nations embodies this ideal — which is precisely the reason why world superpowers, to the present time, keep such tight constricting reins on the power of the UN. It embodies the ideal that one day will become a reality.

(a) **Conventional inherited wisdom** *cherishes monolithic paradigms of knowing and acting, with a clear chain of command from the top down.*

(b) **Embedded codependence** *states that without such linear, patriarchal structures, anarchy would reign supreme. Consequently, from a very young age all citizens are indoctrinated into passive subservience.*

(c) **Adult empowerment** *is not about wrecking or abandoning the major institutions we know (many are already self-destroying), but rather softening the rigid boundaries and deconstructing rigid lines of control, to birth more flexible, creative, and mutually empowering networks, as envisaged in the United Nations dream of the NGO.*

Chapter Six

Theology from the Bottom Up

FOCUS: Theology for most of Christendom belonged to an exclusive male elite and was used to impose control on the "unruly" masses. Today, theology has broken loose from its clerical moorings and is rapidly becoming an interdisciplinary empowering wisdom accessed by millions of adults around the world.

Vernacular theology is engaged theology whose primary approach is through historical consciousness, spirituality, and dialogue. Rather, it is doing theology by way of spirituality.
— ILIA DELIO

THEOLOGY HAS a long imperial history. Dominated by men (clerics) from earliest times, it wholeheartedly embraced the metaphysics, epistemology, and rationality of Greek philosophy. Cerebral clarity held an honored place. And after the collusion with Constantine in the fourth century, Roman imperialism infiltrated every fiber of theological discourse. By the time of Thomas Aquinas, in the thirteenth century, not only was theology the queen of the sciences; it was the king of all knowledge, sacred and secular alike.

It did not err; it could not err. And those who were deemed to be in theological error paid for their deviancy — with fire and sword. Occasionally women broke into the sacred male domain and usually paid a harsh price for doing so. But in the Catholic Church, from the Council of Trent (in the sixteenth century) onward, they could not break in. A new exclusion zone was put in place: the council stated unambiguously and categorically that theology was strictly reserved to priests and priests-to-be. That regulation remained solidly in force until the mid-twentieth century.

Although other Christian denominations did not adopt the rigid exclusion of Catholicism, women also fared poorly in other churches. All religious institutions adopted, to one degree or another, the misogynist suspicion, initially voiced by Aristotle and endorsed by Thomas Aquinas (among many others), that females were misbegotten males, to whom one did not entrust anything of a serious nature, and certainly not something as "powerful" as theological wisdom.

Worthy of note too is the reservation of theology to Christian faith; all other religions were effectively deemed to be pagan rituals to be suppressed and destroyed. Judaism and Islam, because they also espoused the monolithic deity, were accorded more favorable attention. Only in the mid-twentieth century, did Christian churches acknowledge the religious validity of the other great faiths, but to this day they are given only minimal recognition as fully fledged religious systems.

The Paradigm Shift

In 1963 for the first time ever, Sisters (nuns) were admitted to Heythrop College (then in Oxford, UK) to study theology. They were emphatically informed that this vast concession was granted to equip them to be more effective religion teachers in schools and parishes. Consequently, they would be granted a bachelor's degree in theology and immediately would proceed to use their newly accumulated wisdom in their various ministries. Under no circumstances could they pursue further studies in theology or scripture; that privilege was reserved for priests or priests-to-be.

By 1970, the new paradigm had taken its quantum leap, an inconspicuous trickle that was to become a powerful stream, indeed a full-flowing river, within a mere decade. We reckon that of all theologians in the Catholic Church in 1970, nonpriests comprised about 5 percent. By 1980, it would register 25 percent, with the first nonpriests teaching theology in the early 1980s. Today, we estimate that at least 60 percent of all theologians in the Catholic Church are lay people (nonclerics). The priest theologian is now a declining species. The paradigm is gone past the point of no return.

Ilia Delio (2008, 124–25), describes this new theological horizon as vernacular theology. Its language is born out of the experience of the ordinary, rather than the extraordinary, intuitive wisdom from the bottom up, rather than imposed from on high. It is grounded in the world of daily experience rather than on the reified wisdom of academic enclaves. And as Vigil et al. (2010) illustrate, its discerning focus is the search for spiritual meaning within the planetary and cosmic context of creation rather than the achievement of salvation in a world beyond. In the words of Elizabeth Johnson (quoted in Cannato 2006, 135):

> A flourishing humanity on a thriving Earth in an evolving universe, all together filled with the glory of God — such is the theological vision and praxis we are being called to in this critical age of Earth's distress.

Like most paradigm shifts, we cannot detect a trigger mechanism. Nobody set out to make it happen. Ecclesiastical forces certainly did not encourage it; even to this day there are clerics in the Catholic Church who do not acknowledge the shift that has taken place. It feels safer to keep one's head buried in the sands of denial and ignorance.

There are important features to this breakthrough, with significant implications for adult faith development now and for the future.

1. *Theology is no longer reserved to the academic domain.* Millions of Christians read and study theology. Many engage easily in religious theological discourse. People openly disagree with long-held beliefs and question what seem to be time-honored positions. Ethically and morally, a declining percentage of people look to churches or to formal religions for guidance; instead, they consult with peers and colleagues and trust their own insight and intuition. Theology is rapidly becoming a field for intellectual exploration — *intellectual* but not necessarily *academic* — to which many "nontheologians" bring their adult insights and interpretative questions.

2. *Theology has gone global, even beyond the boundaries acknowledged in multifaith dialogue.* For long, theology has been considered

a sacred discipline in which faith seeks deeper understanding. For much of the Christian era, the search was postulated on the solid unquestioned truth of the deposit of revelation as embodied in the Christian scriptures. Faith, in effect, translated into espousing the contents of the Nicean Creed (drawn up at the Council of Nicea in 325 C.E.). In the closing decades of the twentieth century, a small group of theologians explored links with the great religions of Asia in an attempt to integrate their insights into theological discourse. The endeavor ran into theological bottlenecks, not least the inherited fixed understanding of revelation. Already by the dawn of the twenty-first century, the movement had lost a good deal of its initial enthusiasm.

Meanwhile, a rising generation of lay people espouse and explore interfaith collaboration. There prevails today a broad understanding of what the various religions represent, their differences, and, of increasing significance, their *commonalities*. How the religions can be used to bring us together, rather than hold us apart, is what engages and excites people of adult faith in our time (see King 2009; Vigil et al. 2010). This is not merely a conceptual exploration, reviewing what theological notions like incarnation or revelation might mean in different faith traditions; rather the focus is the common strands that awaken justice and empowerment to address urgent contemporary questions (e.g., environment, nonviolence, oppression, marginalization) and forge a common strategy to transcend traditional barriers to dialogue, peace, and harmony.

3. *Theology has become quite multidisciplinary and interdisciplinary.* The academic world generally is still heavily committed to mono-disciplinary analysis. As in our school systems, we tend to keep various subjects in neat conceptual boxes: math, biology, history, religion, sociology, etc. However, the consciousness of our time is shifting rapidly toward multidisciplinary and interdisciplinary understandings. In fact, it is widely accepted that most of the pressing issues confronting humanity today — environmental, economic, political — cannot be addressed effectively without an interdisciplinary strategy.

A great deal of lay-inspired theology is already flourishing in this ambience. Our information-saturated world evokes a desire to make more and more connections — across disciplines and various fields of study. Adult people of faith tend to move in this direction and rejoice in the multifarious enrichment that ensues. For this new generation, theology does not and cannot stand alone; it needs to be in interactive and interpretative dialogue with other disciplines, e.g., theology and economics (McFague 2001), theology, science, and evolutionary theory (Dowd 2008); theology and technology (Waters 2006); theology, ecology, and cosmology (Hathaway and Boff 2009).

4. *Lay theologians do theology in a vastly different way from their clerical counterparts.* Even to this day, priest theologians tend to be selected, not just for intellectual brilliance, but because they are perceived as being loyal and faithful to ecclesiastical tradition and wisdom. And there are some priest theologians, while thinking well outside the box, still try to safeguard the inherited wisdom and integrate it with newly emerging wisdom.

Lay people who study theology in seminaries or universities obviously inherit this clerical overlay to one degree or another. Some regard it suspiciously from the start, and by the time they graduate they are often doing theology in the context of the world rather than of the church. Of course some lay people will cling on rigidly to the inherited tradition, but overall a strong ferment is emerging indicating that lay people do theology very differently from priests. The latter are preoccupied with the primacy of the church; the former strive to do theology in the context of our rapidly changing world.

It is not my intention to create a divisive polarization between priest and lay theologian. I highlight the distinction in the hope of avoiding an unhealthy polarization. There seems to be little dialogue between these two groups, each with its own insights and understandings. It feels like few if any want to acknowledge the growing gap, whereby an increasing percentage of lay people follow the wider, more "secular" view of the lay theologian, progressively sidelining the influence of the priest theologian. The evolutionary outcome, however, seems in little doubt: the lay theologian will outpace and outlive the priest theologian and will win a wider credibility particularly among the spiritual seekers in our emerging globalized cultures.

5. *Radicalizing Christian Theology.* For much of the Christian era, theology's primary function was perceived as passing on the truths

of Christian faith, based on the revelation of scripture and inculturated in the teaching and liturgy of formal Christian churches. That focus changed significantly throughout the twentieth century, as Christian theologians sought to realign Christian faith with one pervasive theme of the Christian Gospels: The New Reign of God (Kingdom of God). That iconic image came to be understood as the primary focus of the teaching and ministry of Jesus and therefore was deemed to be the core dimension of all authentic Christian life and teaching.

Seeking to honor the original Aramaic in which Jesus spoke, some scholars suggest that a more accurate and responsible translation of the "Kingdom of God" (heaven) is that of *the companionship of empowerment* (see O'Murchu 2009, 32–35). This rendering embodies two key elements: Christian life is about *empowerment,* and is therefore called to be a counterculture to all forms of destructive power; second, the envisaged empowerment is facilitated not by some new benign form of hierarchical mediation, but by *dynamic creative communities* — described in Part Two of this book as the power of *networking.*

Re-visioning theology as the servant wisdom of the companionship of empowerment radically changes not merely the inherited meaning but the prophetic horizon of the theological enterprise. Indeed, theology once more becomes a subversive dangerous memory, unambiguously committed to liberty from all oppressions and to empowerment for that fullness of life to which all creatures are called (see John 10:10). Its appeal for contemporary adults will be explored in Part Two.

Theological Confidence

The lay person's excursus into the realm of theology exemplifies a sense of self-confidence that is central to the emergence of adult faith in the twenty-first century. Faith is no longer identified as a resource humans need to compensate for their sin and waywardness in order to win God's good favor and the gift of eternal life. Increasingly faith is perceived to be a divine-human, cocreative adventure, calling forth adult men and women to engage as fully as possible in the transformative task of establishing the Kingdom of God on earth.

Fundamentalist (sometimes described as "evangelical") faith and theology cannot cope with this adult maturity. They denounce it as humans playing God, alleging that such people underestimate the depravity of the human condition and buy too easily into the destructive culture of postmodernism. For some conventional scripture scholars and theologians, this new sense of faith among lay people is denounced as eschatologically weak: the ultimate triumph of God's goodness and judgment is underrated, and even neglected.

Lay people of more mature faith certainly embrace a very different sense of divine ultimacy. Talk about the end of the world makes little or no sense in this new adult faith ferment. Lay theologians embrace more readily the insights of modern science and cosmology, viewing creation's evolution in a story of billions of years and not merely a few millennia. This enlarged time scale is also attractive because it helps to highlight the expansiveness of God's creativity in the world. Even if creation is destined for some ultimate end, it will not happen for billions of years yet to come.

Speculation about the end of the world is viewed by this new generation of theologians (and reflective Christians in general) as preposterous scare-mongering, valuable in earlier times to make sense out of intense suffering and persecution, but today an empty rhetoric based on irrational fear, thriving on human insecurity, alienating more reflective people, and offering little meaningful hope for our turbulent times. It can also distract from the more imminent apocalyptic doom — for the human species itself heading blindly toward self-extinction unless we drastically change our ways.

The contemporary lay theologian seeks to address the here-and-now of evolutionary creation, seeking to discern the call of God in the face of the major issues facing us as an earth-based species, seeking to understand what the Kingdom of God means, or could mean, in our times, and striving to respond in an adult responsible way as cocreators with our creative God. Whatever our human limitations — and the lay theologian acknowledges these every bit as much as any traditional Christian — God is on our side. And God seeks us out as collaborative friends in the great cosmic and earthly drama of evolutionary becoming.

How it will all end, and the ultimate destiny of each one of us, is not of any real interest to the lay theologians of our time. *Engagement* and not *escape* is the crucial issue. Humans have often ignored and even maligned God's creation — and therefore tried to hinder God's creative endeavor — hoping one day to elope from this vale of tears to the utopia beyond the sky. Now we need to take creation seriously as God's primary revelation for us and work convivially and collaboratively to further the evolutionary growth into greater complexity, so necessary to preserve and enhance the grandeur of both God and humankind on this earth.

Theological Bridge-Building

Lay theology casts a wide net within a contextual landscape (see Pears 2009). It embraces commonalities rather than differences and seeks dialogue with every person and movement, desiring to build a better world, where justice and love can flourish. To understand and do justice to the complexities of modern life, lay theologians adopt multidisciplinary insight and analysis. They seek dialogue with partners in various fields of learning, transcending wherever possible the dualistic distinction between the sacred and the secular. In this way, theology offers the exciting prospect of becoming the most interdisciplinary of all the sciences. It may even become a prototype for interdisciplinary intellectual enrichment.

This enlarged intellectual horizon requires not merely peer supervision and support, usually deemed to be essential to multidisciplinary research, but also regular *professional spiritual discernment*. In the conventional paradigm it is assumed that discernment is not necessary, apart from peer supervision. That scripture scholars or theologians should avail themselves of regular spiritual direction is virtually unheard of in standard Christian theology. Without such recourse to spiritual accompaniment, the theologian of the future runs the risk of failing to discern creatively the new horizons to which the Spirit forever lures. Scholarly competence needs to be matched with in-depth spiritual insight and wisdom.

Pastoral application of theological insight also requires new skills, especially for cross-cultural discernment. Traditional devotional practices still dominate in the Christian world, particularly among the poor and marginalized. These devotions certainly empower people struggling to survive in some appalling conditions. It is comforting and consoling to bombard heaven, supplicating God's mercy and love, simply in order to survive and endure. The rich also resort to such popular devotion, hoping to advance their personal prosperity in this life, and eternal salvation in the next.

Both lay and clerical theologians are acutely aware of the enormous gap that often exists between the liberating power of theological vision and the entrapment that can ensue from a faith largely based on devotional practices. Millions in Africa resort to popular devotions to cope with the trauma and loss ensuing from HIV/AIDS, yet such practices do little or nothing to address the horrendous injustices whereby it took Africans so long to get access to retroviral drugs with which AIDS sufferers in other parts of the planet could live reasonably wholesome lives. Not merely did the devotions do little to procure justice and something akin to Gospel liberation, but worse still such devotions often confounded people into thinking that what they were enduring and suffering was God's will for them and that they would be all the better for it.

This is what I describe as theological bridge-building, a challenge that lay theologians in particular and people seeking to appropriate a more adult sense of faith, are acutely aware of. I find the following distinction helpful:

- *The devotion of consolation:* particularly when exploring pastoral theological guidelines, we need to be sensitive to the millions who cry out in both despair and hope, using what may seem like infantile methods of prayer and devotion. In oppressive circumstances, all of us are likely to resort to such devotional spirituality; the urge to survive is deeply rooted in all our hearts. We do not have the right to tread brutally on that which is sacred to people already crushed, vulnerable, and dis-spirited by a brutal world. And yet, to be theologically responsible, we know we cannot let people remain at that level, because that is effectively condemning them to further oppression, injustice, and degradation.

♦ *The spirituality of liberation:* every religion aspires toward an inner freedom that seeks expression in our external way of living. "Set my people free" is inscribed in the vision of all the great religions in one form or another. Unfortunately, many of the religions short-circuit their own vision by projecting this hunger for freedom to a utopian state beyond this present world. At least from the Christian point of view, the ultimate goal of faith is the freedom to grow into that fullness of life which God desires for all peoples. This also becomes the pastoral theological goal that must not be compromised. And people of adult faith feel called to honor that priority.

Obviously, the pastoral resolution is about both-and and not either-or. Serious discernment, however, leaves us in no doubt as to which option must be prioritized: the spirituality of liberation! Theologically, we are called to befriend people through their pain and struggles in devotional solidarity, while seeking every opportunity to assist and empower people to transcend the devotional supports and mobilize their creative energy to bring about systemic and structural change so that justice can be released and people's lives transformed into more wholesome ways of living.

In this enterprise, there is no room for dualistic divisions, especially between the sacred and the secular, nor is the endeavor merely about people in isolation. Systemic factors, particularly those of political and economic import, have to be included, confronted, and addressed. More urgently still are the pressing ecological and environmental issues that undermine not merely human dignity, but the very viability of the living earth itself, so essential for healthy development of every organism that cohabits the planet with us.

Ecojustice is not merely a response to urgent issues like global warming and environmental degradation; it is the type of justice through which we seek to treat every life form with greater respect and freedom; otherwise, all are condemned to oppression and ruination.

Theology, long regarded as being the queen of the sciences, is rapidly outgrowing its clerical ecclesiastical enclave, where it was often used to keep people, particularly adults, in obedient submission. Today, it is poised to become one of the most creative, proactive, and empowering of all disciplines, with a credibility staked on making the New Reign of God more visible and liberating on the face of the living earth.

(a) **Conventional inherited wisdom** *considers theology to be a divinely bestowed power for knowing the will of God through fidelity to the institutionalized understanding of the faith as embodied in the traditional interpretation of Holy Writ.*

(b) **Embedded codependency** *prioritizes rational reasoning, with which primarily men are endowed, as the greatest guarantee that truth will be preserved, thus ensuring that power and control are in the hands of the most trusted members.*

(c) **Adult empowerment** *is somewhat akin to breaking the cycle of slavery or victimization, asserting one's legitimate place at the table of theological dialogue, and bringing forth those enlarged, alternative insights that have long been kept subdued.*

Part Two

Horizons of
Quantum Possibility

Life tends to optimize rather than maximize.
— PAUL HAWKEN

*I cast my lot with those who, age after age, perversely, with no
extraordinary power, reconstitute the world.*
— ADRIENNE RICH

PART TWO is an attempt at reconstruction, not beginning with
a blank slate but embracing and endorsing a transformation
already well under way:

- Since the middle of the twentieth century human evolution has
  moved with greater rapidity, as a new understanding of what
  constitutes the human has been evolving. The implications for
  what it means to be adult in this new unfolding still await serious
  study and analysis.

- Adult faith development has been gaining recognition and credibility ever since the seminal work of James Fowler in the 1970s.
  It now needs a more public and formal endorsement.

- Disillusionment with formal religion, and the search for a
  more vibrant spirituality, engage adults of our time on a
  crosscultural basis.

• New insights from science and cosmology impact strongly on today's emerging spirituality (see Cannato 2006; 2010). The new worldview captivates the spiritual imagination of growing numbers of adults on a worldwide scale.

• The emerging spirituality seeks a greater integration based on justice and mutual empowerment for every living creature inhabiting planet earth. Because mainstream political and economic institutions are slow to move in this direction, a widespread disillusionment with major institutions characterizes our time. Adults seek more creative alternatives, networking being one of the more promising options.

• In amorphous and at times chaotic ways, a new adult spiritual awakening is taking place. Coherent articulations are still in the future. Hopefully the reflections of this book will help pave the way toward clarity and greater conviction for those embracing this new vision.

Chapter Seven

Calling Forth the Adult
in the Twenty-First Century

FOCUS: Adulthood in earlier times denoted a quality of maturation, engagement, and achievement, very much seen as a male heroic task. Coevolution is birthing a new stage in adulthood, with a kind of multiple personality, flourishing through relational interaction with multiple others, human and nonhuman alike.

Humanity in this new era needs to be renegotiated, updated, and made heroic. The time has come for the maturation of our collective soul. — JASON HILL

THE CLOSING DECADES of the twentieth century marked breakthroughs that few could have anticipated. To the fore was the information explosion, awakening a new sense of global interconnectedness. In turn this led to a more aggressive globalization of trade and commerce, with the corporate world going transnational as sanctioned by the launch of the WTO (World Trade Organization) in 1994. In just a few decades worldwide travel increased fourfold; with passion and excitement people began to embrace the new global freedom.

However, all was not well in the new global order, and that was vividly portrayed in the attack on New York's twin towers on September 11, 2001; the American Empire was more vulnerable than many had suspected. Meanwhile in the Southern Hemisphere, HIV/AIDS began to reap havoc, while violence, war, and ethnic rivalries cost millions of human lives. The hole in the ozone layer faded into the background but instead global warming became the new ecological crisis of the early twenty-first century. Despite the euphoria that can be traced back to the 1960s, humans were not making a good job of the planetary project entrusted to their care. To the contrary many feared we were entering a new era of human regression, and scholars true to form came up with new philosophical explanations.

Out of Modernity

The complex, evolving landscape of the modern world, outlined briefly in the opening paragraphs above, has an impact on our self-understanding and self-definition as a human species. We become different people under the impact of new cultural demands. Novel potentialities are being evoked in our inner beings and called forth in how we deal with reality. For adults in particular our identity is undergoing seismic shifts. At times, it feels like a new creature is coming into being. And scholarly opinion varies widely as we try to make sense of what is transpiring at this time.

Many specialists employ a development known as *postmodernism* to help explain what is emerging.[4] It seeks to name a new freedom, with individualism, relativism, and fluidity among its core elements. Postmodernism sets out to critique and redefine what for long we accepted as the "essentials" of human nature. It calls into question the anthropology of an earlier period broadly known as *modernity*.

Modernity is fundamentally about order: dealing with rationality and rationalization, creating order out of chaos. The assumption is that creating more rationality is conducive to creating more order, and that the more ordered a society is, the better it will function. Thus societal culture is maintained through a series of *grand narratives* to which everybody is expected to subscribe, a series of core truths that are essentially beyond question.

Postmodernism calls into question the following defining features of being an adult:

1. There is a stable, coherent, knowable self. This self is conscious, rational, autonomous, and universal; it is the ideal to which everybody should aspire.

2. This self knows itself and the world through *reason*, or rationality, posited as the highest form of mental functioning, and essential for objective verification of all truth.

3. The mode of knowing produced by the objective rational self is *science,* which can provide universal truths about the world, regardless of the individual status of the knower.

4. The knowledge produced by science is *truth,* considered to be eternal. That eternal truth of life is what religion describes as *theology.*

5. The knowledge/truth produced by science (by the rational, objective, knowing self) will always lead toward progress and perfection. All human institutions and practices can be analyzed by science (reason/objectivity) and improved as the need arises.

6. *Reason* is the ultimate judge of what is true, right, and good (legally and ethically). Freedom consists of *obedience to the laws* that conform to the knowledge discovered by reason. Theology adds: and God is the source of all objective truth, which can be accessed from the revelation embodied in scripture.

7. In a world governed by reason, the true will always be the same as the good and the right (and the beautiful); there can be no conflict between what is true and what is right.

8. Science thus stands as the paradigm for any and all socially useful forms of knowledge. Theology adopts these same principles but because of its closer affiliation with God, the ultimate source of truth, then theology deems itself as superior to rational science.

9. *Language,* or the mode of expression used in producing and disseminating knowledge, must be rational also. To be rational, language must be transparent; it must function only to represent the real/perceivable world that the rational mind observes. Theologically, this often leads to a literal interpretation of scripture.

These are some of the fundamental premises of modernity. They serve to justify and explain virtually all of our contemporary social structures and institutions, including democracy, law, science, ethics, aesthetics, and most importantly, *capitalism*. Any deviation from such master narratives leads to relativism, perceived as a sure road to perdition by those guarding the ordered reality.

It seems to me that postmodernity is quite clear about what it wishes to reject: a relatively stable, rational, ordered sense of being human. As an alternative, it envisages a humanity characterized by fluidity, flexibility, impermanence, distrust and suspicion of all that is fixed and formally structured. It perceives this emergence as a fact of our time, not necessarily a desirable development, but one in which we don't have any choice. We either accept and embrace it, or otherwise remain stuck in the more monolithic model of modernity.

Religiously and philosophically, postmodernism is often denounced because it leads to fragmentation, provisionality, performance, and instability. Clarity and security are felt to be under severe strain. Truth can be interpreted as anybody feels like it. And this way of believing poses an enormous threat for conventional authority in both the secular and religious domains.

Postmodernism is essentially a philosophical movement, rendering a reading of reality that is nuanced, yet superficial, with particular appeal to academics (predominantly males). It is extensively evoked by those who bemoan the loss of modernity with its key values of stability, predictability, structure, order, along with clarity on who was in charge. This led to a very clear concept of the adult with strong emphasis on *gender* and *social function:*

1. Civic responsibility exercised mainly through employment — holding down a regular job.

2. Domestic responsibility exercised through monogamous, heterosexual marriage, which normally required creating one's own home.

3. Cultural responsibility exercised through procreation of new life and the furtherance of the patriarchal culture through the institution of the family.

In this earlier model of modernity, the sexist undertones are all too obvious. Males, and males only, can become adult, in the fuller sense of adult achievement. The exercise of patriarchal power requires a quality of rationality and resilience that is assumed to be far more developed in males than in females. Remnants of this misogyny still prevail in some major institutions of our time, excluding females from various realms of employment and social interaction where males are prioritized; in some cases males are the only ones who are admitted. Echoes of this same oppressive exclusion are manifest in the Catholic Church's prohibition on the ordination of women. No matter what religious rhetoric may be invoked to justify such an arrangement, it cuts little ice for the more informed adults today.

Such patriarchal values tend to be embedded in, and supported by, national governments, cultural institutions such as schools, social services, and health facilities, and finally by religious systems some of which are unashamedly hierarchical and domineering, and others more subtle but nonetheless prioritizing the male patriarchal hege-mony. In such contexts people take identity, value, and enhancement from the successful achievement of assigned tasks and the mean-ingful participation in the cultural institutions accompanying such endeavors.

The entire package is subtly but strongly controlled, and deviations are dealt with promptly and effectively. Rewards and punishments feature strongly in this system. External measurements far exceed anything to do with internal feelings or emotions. People are judged by how effectively they perform the task assigned to them.

This system began to fragment seriously in the 1960s. Young people particularly rebelled against the formality and rigidity of the prevailing cultural norms. The reactive element was quite clear; the proactive dimension was often quite vague. What alternative lifestyle were they actually seeking? That continues to be a fundamental question for humanity today.

One attempt to redress the patriarchal imbalance — often cited by modern philosophers (e.g., Hill 2009, 92ff) — is to establish *key capabilities* without which humans cannot live with dignity or integrity.

In the oft cited works of Martha Nussbaum (2001; 2007) governments and religions are challenged to uphold ten capabilities deemed essential for a human-fulfilling existence. The list includes the basic right to life and to the resources to live life in a worthwhile way. Contrary to some patriarchal approaches, strong emphasis rests on the use and development of intuition, imagination, and emotion, along with facilities for empowering socialization and political engagement (see *http://people.wku.edu/jan.garrett/nussbaum.htm*).

Characteristics of Contemporary Adulthood

Institutionally and organizationally, millions around our world still operate within the culture of modernity. Most of our major institutions provide a top-down structure, with the few in charge and the many cast into various codependent roles. At that level it seems as if little has changed. Yet we know that as a species we are undergoing substantial transformations in our understanding of reality, our perceptions and our values. A growing chasm between our ways of seeing and our ways of doing characterizes our experience today. This is the catalyst calling forth the new adult identity described below.

The Internet provides numerous lists outlining the characteristics of a new paradigm of adulthood. These typically include the ability to manage emotions more constructively, to operate with greater self-confidence, and to enhance one's personal development consistently, without exploiting or damaging other people. These lists tend to exhibit one major deficiency: *they view humans in isolation.* They pay little or no attention to contextual dimensions without which we would not even exist, never mind flourish. The lists reflect our highly anthropocentric inheritance, with the reductionistic set of values that favor the human over everything else in creation. The lists make no links with the embracing web of life, the cosmic, planetary, and spiritual dynamics that shape our existence more pervasively and profoundly than most of us recognize. Without those other dimensions, true adulthood stands little chance of being honored or promoted.

On the following page I have adopted one of the standard lists with a strong anthropocentric focus. I then supplement each characteristic with the larger transpersonal values, thus keeping our portrayal of the human grounded in the wider reality of life. The emerging tapestry of adulthood seeks to honor not merely the wider secular sphere of our existence but also the spiritual influences that help mold and shape a far more rounded way of engaging with the whole of life. Obviously this is an ideal that none of us will ever fully realize, yet it seems to be the alluring horizon inspiring and challenging many adults today.

The older, conventional characteristics (outlined on the left) focus on human growth in relative isolation, with an emphasis on practical daily living. The desired goal is that of the self-reliant, robust individual, the one who can compete effectively in society and make it "for oneself." Although seldom acknowledged, this way of being often leads to boredom and stagnation, a cultural pathology, often characterized by anomie and denial as succinctly described by Hathaway and Boff (2009, 15–126).

The reformulated list (right-hand column) — what I name as the integrated approach — seeks to redeem our personal identity and growth from the enclave of isolated, imperial individualism. It situates the reality of each one of us within the evolving web of life with implications — some of which are vast and wide — that were never considered in the older (conventional) approach. The fact that we are cosmic creatures, planetary beings, relationally programed people, whose identity is defined by *belonging* rather than by *independence or autonomy*, received little attention in former times. When these elements are included, then human growth veers more toward intimacy (not merely with other humans), a much more complex sense of engagement demanding far greater creativity, which in fact arises from an already established integrity (with the entire web of life) and continually reinforces growth toward greater integrity.

ON BEING ADULT

Conventional Values	Evolutionary Values
1. Reaching a voting age, usually at eighteen.	Adulthood may start as early as twelve years of age and is always in process.
2. Learning to think rationally and deal with abstractions.	The integration of the rational, emotional, social, intellectual, and spiritual is the task of an entire lifespan.
3. Fulfilling educational requirements for effective work and citizenship.	Academic achievement is one dimension of intellectual development, and the latter serves goals other than work and citizenship.
4. Managing money effectively.	Money is a means to an end, not a goal in itself.
5. Obtaining a paying job and learning to be a strong competitor.	Work satisfaction means more than good money. Adults prefer work that serves well both the community and the planet.
6. Beginning serious relationships, with a view to marrying and having a family.	The capacity to relate intimately is a lifelong, complex, and multifaceted undertaking. Inherited notions of marriage and family life have lost a great deal of social and cultural significance.
7. Holding your place (power) through meaningful conversations.	Conversations and relationships that mutually empower have stronger appeal for adults in our time.
8. Knowing your rights and protecting those of others.	Adults today cherish rights but also wish to highlight corresponding duties — for person and planet alike.
9. Getting socially involved and exercising civic duties.	Social involvement incorporates persons, communities, the environment and the planet.
10. Using your emotions wisely, and always in a controlled way.	Emotions are complex and need discerning wisdom as well as informed discipline.
11. Distinguishing between "needs" and "wants."	And become aware of the transpersonal influences which are always at work.
12. Following a religion if you find it useful.	Mature religion begets empowering spirituality which cannot be judged merely in terms of functional usefulness.
13. Striving to be happy in yourself.	Happiness is a transpersonal process achieved by soulful engagement with every dimension of the web of life.

The Postmodern, Evolutionary Adult

Eight key principles underline the features of the right-hand column:

1. *Relationality defines identity.* Everything and everybody in creation functions and thrives through a mutual web of relationships. The relationality is not merely about humans relating with other humans, but with every other organism that constitutes the web of cosmic and planetary life.

2. *Human life is inescapably dependent on the cosmos and on planet earth* for its coming into being, survival, and flourishing. Human isolation is meaningless and can only beget meaninglessness.

3. *Humans are programed for mutuality and cooperation,* not for competition and domination of all other life forms. This is the *altruism* that numerous contemporary scholars are exploring afresh (see Dowd 2008; Hrdy 2009; Margulis 1998; Stewart 2000).

4. The *transpersonal* is more pervasive and empowering than the conventional understanding of personhood. We become fully human — especially in our adult unfolding — through our *mutual interdependence* with every other life form. Isolation, independence, and cultural superiority destroy the true potential of humanity (and of every other life form as well).

5. *Process is central* to our evolutionary growth and development. Every point of arrival (e.g., adolescence) marks a departure for the next stage on the journey. The journey never ends, not even in death.

6. *Empowerment* rather than power-seeking, or power mongering, is the most effective strategy to release creative potential not merely in humans but in every dimension of cosmic-planetary life.

7. *Integration* is the goal of all cultural aspirations — what the Christian Gospels call the fullness of life — and cannot be

realized without a vibrant empowering spirituality that may or may not include a formal religion.

8. *Discernment* provides a more reliable pathway to truth than rationality or the rigor of the scientific method. Discerning wisdom draws on a wide spectrum of experience including insight, intuition, imagination, understanding, analysis, dialogue, and spiritual apprehension.[5]

There is a clarity and concreteness about the concept of the adult in former times that no longer endures in our contemporary consciousness, whether defined as modern or postmodern. Today, we strive to honor the evolutionary dynamic indicating that everything in creation is programed to *grow, change, and develop*. Every creature is endowed with the giftedness of creativity, which best flourishes in a climate where openness, fluidity, and flexibility are cherished values.

Throughout Part Two of this book I will use three interchangeable terms to describe the emerging adult in our time: "protean," "cosmopolitan," "coevolutionary." We have already encountered the protean adult (p. 10), described by Mikela and Philip Tarlow (2002, 82) as "a more mature way of coping with competing demands, ambiguities, and complexities of modern life. The self becomes capable of morphing into unlimited shapes in order to connect with the *window* that is before it, virtual or real." Identity is more an ongoing process of discovery rather than a once-off achievement or one that is altered by life changes in work or in relationships.

Second, I use the term "cosmopolitan" as developed by Jamaican-American philosopher Jason Hill (2002; 2009):

Many of us have been living as closeted cosmopolitans. That is, we have been living under the aegis of racism, racialism, nationalism, and excessive and bloated patriotism. Rigid tribal arrangements that even in their informal stances still dominate our conscious lives have acted as formal mores that regulate our civic alliances.... Many of us have longed to live post-ethnic, postracial, and postnational lives, but fear of losing the

> security that accompanies group solidarity (delayed weaning)
> prevents the willed weaning that is a prerequisite for that type
> of "lifestyle." (Hill 2002, 1–2)

Hill describes the gradual breakdown of ethnic differences and distinctions, as peoples of diverse cultural backgrounds encounter and interact with a greater frequency in the modern world. He is also painfully aware of the ideological barriers that prohibit this realization — on quite an extensive scale. Radical though his ideas are, he restricts his analysis to the human domain; he remains within the anthropocentric realm, whereas the present work wishes to resituate the cosmopolitan human in the planetary-cosmic web of life.

And the third naming, *coevolutionary,* seeks to expand and correct what I perceive to be the anthropocentric short-sightedness of the other two namings (protean, cosmopolitan). It denotes, among other things, a more conscious option to live in harmony with the rhythm and flow of the surrounding creation. In this context, our humanity is not viewed in anthropocentric isolation, but as belonging intimately to the cosmic and planetary web of life. From within this wider, deeper connective web we appropriate a different set of values in our engagements with daily life. We learn to live within a more convivial, organic, interdependent mutuality, gradually letting go of the anthropocentric mastery and the insatiable desire for power so innate to our inherited wisdom.

Science writer Rita Carter (2008) reviews recent neurological research indicating that the human brain has the capacity to morph into a range of personalities as different circumstances demand, described by Gus Gordon (2009, 158) as the "mutational person." Conventional psychology perceives the human personality as a kind of monolithic unity, with an essential core unique to each person. That view has been changing throughout the latter half of the twentieth century as we realize that identity is the fruit of relational interaction rather than arising from isolated individual striving. And the relational web through which we all grow and flourish requires substantial personality changes as we engage with the complex realities of life, even in daily interaction.

Characterized by a sense of fluidity, common in today's world, the *protean, cosmopolitan, coevolutionary* person is reluctant to attach exclusively to any fixed, monolithic identity. Being persons in process, we are invited and challenged to evolve *in a more conscious way* within a web of relationships, broad and deep like the cosmic web of life itself.

The New Consciousness

The vision of the new adulthood outlined in these pages will strike some as quite speculative, naïve, or falsely idealistic. Some will ask: Where is the evidence? Others will feel no need to ask, because I am describing a way of being they know from personal experience. I am depicting quite an amorphous landscape with different people at a range of different levels. The crucial issue seems to be: How conscious are we of what is happening to us as an adult species? And what exactly are we referring to when we use the word "consciousness"?

Consciousness is an elusive and intriguing subject and today embraces a vast spectrum of possible meaning. At one end is the position adopted by scholars like Daniel Dennett (1993), for whom consciousness is a mechanical process, confined to the human brain and related to the interactive behavior of brain units known as *qualia*. In other words, consciousness is caused by how the qualia interact in the human brain.

At the other end is the view that consciousness is a quantum phenomenon belonging primarily to the creation we inhabit. Accordingly, individual consciousness is an inherited quality from the quantum field–influence; in other words, a dimension of the creative universal energy from which everything evolves. David John Chalmers (1996), Erwin Laszlo (1996), Gregg H. Rosenberg (2004), and Galen Strawson (2006) are among specialists who opt for this explanation.

In between is a vast field of research, succinctly summarized in the web page for the Psychology Department of the University of Arizona in the United States: *www.consciousness.arizona.edu/abstracts.htm.* Most researchers focus on the mind-body problem, acknowledging that consciousness is in the mind rather than in the brain, but holding divergent views on how we define or describe *mind*, in terms of the human body, but also possibly related to life-energies beyond the realm of the human personality.

I favor the view that extends our understanding of consciousness toward the larger cosmic, quantum realm. Many people today experience this as an allurement toward larger spheres of understanding, a distrust of reductionist theories and solutions, and the incorporation of a spiritual dimension in our attempts to understand consciousness afresh. This is also the realm where we see a new sense of being adult people trusting our own intuitions, checking out our experiences with peers rather than with experts, embracing multi-disciplinary ways of understanding to comprehend deeper meaning, and frequently embracing spiritual insights in the hope of reaching a deeper and more authentic discernment.

Consciousness still evokes a sense of something quite esoteric, although it is subject to a great deal of rigorous scientific analysis. It essentially denotes *awareness,* and evokes questions on what quality and quantity of awareness are being adopted in the human attempt to understand. Awareness involves study, research, cross-checking outcomes with peers and specialists, but for many adults today it also needs to include *skills for better listening.* This is not merely a case of hearing more clearly, but how best to attend to internal processes of intuition, insight, emotionality, and wisdom of the heart. To this end some specialists consider *a regular meditation practice* to be essential.

The practice of *meditation* — through a range of different strategies — is essentially that of centering and focusing our psychic energy at the inner core of our beings (see Cannato 2010, 115–30). It helps to focus thinking, clarify perception, deepen intuition, and enhance insight. A central conviction prevails — one often ridiculed by the academic world — that the search for human meaning and the pursuit of human growth come from a psychic source within, and are not driven merely by biology or external cultural forces. Carl Jung's theory of the collective unconscious, and its archetypal wisdom, is probably the closest we have to a scientific understanding of this inner realm.

The World Wide Web, and access to information in our current experience, are among the immediate triggers for this new wave of consciousness. But as indicated briefly above, it is a great deal more complex and still subject to intense study and research. Meanwhile, humans continue to coevolve, whether understood in Darwinian terms of natural selection, or in more spiritual terms of allurement toward a different future. A new kind of adult is coming to birth, with novel questions and a desire for wisdom that conventional learning often is unable to provide. It feels as if we are only beginning to understand what constitutes this new being, with the challenges for growth and flourishing it furnishes in our time.

Personal identity today cannot be reduced to an inherited template defined by culture, ethnicity, nationality, or religion. Identity is not so much an inherited endowment, but rather an unceasing process of rediscovery, accelerated by modern evolutionary consciousness. There is a past upon which I build, but always a future calling me forth into a larger horizon of meaning and possibility. I am driven by the past, but lured by the future — what the American philosopher Susan Neiman describes as "a grown-up idealist" (Neiman 2009). I cannot escape being a person-in-process. Cosmopolitanism is "risk-taking and favors wide, loose, and overlapping communities, multiple selves, and fluidity within universal human limits" (Hill 2002, 197).

Personality, therefore, is not a fixed phenomenon. Even at the physical level, I am continuously changing as I grow and develop; what we can observe and quantify at the physical level is merely the external expression of a transformative process that becomes ever more complex and profound as we move inwardly. And it is an interiority of cosmic proportions, articulated succinctly in several of the written works of the late Thomas Berry:

> Our sense of who we are and what our role is must begin where the universe begins. . . . Each being in its subjective depths carries the numinous mystery whence the universe emerges into being. (Berry 2009, 120–21)

In the next chapter, I review the educational dynamics that need to be invoked if we are to honor this newly emerging sense of human identity — an *education for liberation* rather than "education as domestication" (Paulo Friere). Educational strategies such as the Steiner method are known to affect children differently than those employed in mainline educational establishments. My interest in the present work is the adult, rather than the child, particularly as more and more lifelong learners participate in educational processes. How we coeducate the coevolutionary person for this time, and for the future, is a challenge that needs our devoted and urgent attention.

(a) *Conventional inherited wisdom views authentic adulthood as a postadolescent time when one can function effectively and (re)productively in the human task of mastering creation.*

(b) *Embedded codependency defines identity by function, measures growth by prowess and achievement, and tends to measure success by external benchmarks. Those who don't measure up are deemed to be failures.*

(c) *Adult empowerment considers humans as highly complex, evolutionary creatures, whose identity and creativity consistently unfold in conjunction with the transpersonal awakenings evoked by evolution itself. We build on the past but for the greater part our development is determined by the lure of the open-ended future.*

Chapter Eight

Transformative Learning
for the Protean Adult

FOCUS: Adults grappling with a new coevolutionary sense of identity learn in ways that are very different from those employed in formal systems of education. Participatory, interactive strategies that enhance and empower adult flourishing are the necessary ingredients.

In order to come home to ourselves, we should realize that what we really need is a radical reeducation from head to toe.
— GUS GORDON

THE EMERGENCE OF the protean self in our time is not merely a cultural rebellion against past oppressive conditioning. Neither is it some new-age craze, nor is it based on some postmodern relativism. It is very much an outcome of the global transformation that is happening all around us. Such emergence cannot be reduced to some simplistic analysis, whether provided by pop psychology, traditional religion, or conventional secular wisdom.

Nor can we simply attribute such new developments to the desire to transcend the cultural dynamics that defined and shaped our past. These have been briefly reviewed in Part One. Traditional ways of being and living are not being deliberately rejected (in most cases). Rather they have lost their appeal, because in evolutionary terms they have outlived their usefulness.

Evolutionary Readiness

The process of evolution is not driven by some mechanical exertion, material or biological, but by the energy of cosmic intelligence (Laszlo

1996). Action follows thought; as we think so we act. But the quality, and quantity, of our thought does not arise merely from the human brain. The *mind* is greater than the *brain*. The human mind is interconnected with the great cosmic consciousness of the universe. More accurately, the human mind is derived from the intelligence that characterizes the entire web of life. And our wisdom flourishes when it embraces and enhances the lure of our evolutionary universe. In our time, this quality of collaboration is often described as *coevolution*.

Coevolution is closely linked with the notion of emergence (see Morowitz 2002; Clayton and Davies 2006), highlighting the complex interactive dynamics through which things grow and flourish. It belongs to a different set of inspirational agents. We are dealing with a more complex world in the throes of huge evolutionary awakening. Another quality of wisdom is required, capable of embracing and engaging the enlarged horizons of meaning that are evolving today in our time. Evolution itself is awakening in us capacities that challenge us to interact in new ways. This awakening has given birth to the *protean, cosmopolitan* self, more fluid, flexible, and prone to collaborate within the cultural matrix of this new evolutionary moment.

Both quantum physics and contemporary studies on the nature of consciousness provide crucial insights for an understanding of this cultural breakthrough. The linear sequential dynamic, based on cause-and-effect progression, is no longer an adequate explanatory tool. Today we are bombarded by quantum leaps. Life moves at a pace we cannot embrace from within the former patriarchal stronghold from which we assumed we could manage and control every eventuality. Patriarchal control is a relic of a dying past. Humans today must learn to trust a wisdom greater than themselves, leading us forth in a complex endeavor that defies linear logic and the capabilities of the rational mind that have guided us over the past few thousand years.

The spatial implications of quantum theory are even more formidable than the linear dynamics of the classical worldview.[6] In our space-time continuum, dynamic activity happens in new interactive configurations and not merely in piecemeal combinations. "The whole is greater than the sum of the parts" has become the new guiding principle of our age. Everything in creation, humans included, belongs to a relational matrix greater than itself. The individual identity of each constituent element is not self-derived or self-delivered, but obtained interactively (and interdependently) from the greater "entangled" whole. Isolation and separation — what classical science calls discrete elements — are no longer the key values; relationality and connectivity are.

Truth and authenticity are no longer based on allegiance to dogmatic assertion, whether religious or cultural. Truth is in creation rather than in human brains. It is based on that which unfolds as we embrace the web of belonging from which we derive everything that empowers us to engage with life. Persons are planetary creatures of cosmic origin. We don't come into the world; rather we come out of it. And we bring with us a deep inherited wisdom empowering us not merely to cope with the exigencies of daily life, but to grapple with the great mysteries that characterize our global embodied existence.

The protean self is inescapably relational: I *am at all times the sum of my relations*, and that's what defines and confers my identity. And that identity is not static, but forever coming into being. That is how it always has been and, paradoxically, that is how we, humans, seem to have understood ourselves for most of our long evolutionary journey of 7 million years. Catherine Keller (2008, 130) provides a cryptic overview: "I become who I will be within the network of relations, rooting in the non-human, blooming in the intimate, branching into the unknown."

Faced with a world of so much cruel pain and suffering, it is hard to accept this rather idealistic utopian portrayal of the human condition. Humanity today seems to be inundated in perversity, and struggles to dream and maintain any vision that offers meaning and hope. At the present time it is difficult to identify even a single collective example where we get it right. Understandably, some people wonder if creation might be better off without us, so deviant and destructive we have become as a planetary species. That observation also provides the clue to a possible way forward, one frequently alluded to in the pages of this book.

It seems that we got it right for much of our long evolutionary history. In our engagement with creation, in our collaborative endeavor with the other life forms that shared the planet with us, we proved to be creative, productive, and amazingly nonviolent for most of the time. The vital clue seems to be: *closeness to nature.* When we, humans, adopt a convivial relationship with the rest of creation we prove to be the spectacular creatures our inner wisdom often likes to claim. And the corollary is painful to see: when we regard the rest of creation as an object for our use and exploitation, we become destructive monsters, progressively plunging ourselves into anomie and alienation.

The big conversion to which we are all called is not to God or religion — at least not as understood in contemporary cultures. The conversion is to something much more foundational: reclaim the cosmic and planetary womb of our origins and develop afresh convivial and collaborative skills with creation as a living organism, and not as some kind of dead inert matter. This more organic worldview needs to become a central feature of all learning and adaptation for our future. On it depends both our sanity and our sanctity.

The Transformative Nexus

In the present context the word "transformation" essentially denotes *change,* permanent change, and change that endures. It is in our ability to change *continuously* that we grow and flourish. When we emphasize our static place in the scheme of things, we tend to veer toward dogmatism, domination, and violent manipulation of everything we encounter. Change, on the other hand, keeps us supple, fluid, and open to the new. It challenges our compulsion to play God. It keeps us humble (from *humus = earth*), and more closely aligned to our planetary and cosmic foundations.

Transformation in its deeper meaning seeks to embrace this foundational wisdom. It denotes a quality and quantity of change, within and around us, a change that impacts upon us, above and beyond our own control. It is about the wisdom we need to negotiate wisely what transpires as we journey in a quantum, fluctuating, entangled universe. It is the awakening and awareness that life happens to us as much as we invent it. And that our best inventions tend to transpire as we embrace and trust the evolutionary process to which we belong.[7]

What does *education* mean against this background? More specifically, what would a transformative model of *adult education* look like? A transformative model of education tends to be associated with the pioneering work of people like Jean Piaget and Maria Montessori. Their primary interest was in the education of children. In the 1970s, Jack Mezirow did a study of women who had returned to education as adults, suggesting that a new approach was needed, embracing some key principles already adopted by Montessori, Piaget, and others. The new method came to be known as *Learning as Transformation.*[8]

Adults bring a vast range of experience to the learning environment and learn best when that experience is acknowledged and integrated. This is best achieved through a collaborative endeavor where teacher and learner adopt mutual roles based on shared wisdom and where dialogue is the normal opus operandi. The teacher becomes a resource person or facilitator for a shared wisdom rather than being the dispenser of "superior" knowledge to largely passive recipients. The principles guiding adult transformative learning, or what Patricia Cranton (2006) describes as *emancipatory knowledge,* are inherently practical, even for everyday living.

1. Adults bring to the learning context reservoirs of *experience,* all of which is informative and much of which is transformative. Theory needs to be checked out and tested against experience. Experience is a reservoir of deep wisdom.

2. To access the experience we must first trust it, then embrace it, and through reflection and dialogue discern its deeper messages. "Emancipatory knowledge," writes Patricia Cranton (2006, 13), "is gained through a process of critically questioning ourselves and the social systems within which we live."

3. Embracing experience and honoring its deeper wisdom is difficult against the inherited cultural background dominated by dualistic division and subject to excessive rational discourse.

The grip of this conditioning needs to be loosened; we still encounter adult learners who want simple factual answers, thus excusing them from having to think for themselves and work things out in a more reflective adult way.

4. *Skills for critical reflection* are central to this process. Critical vigilance around dogmatic impositions, excessive rationalism, monolithic truth (there can be only one right way) and inherited assumptions is seen as normative and healthy. The collective wisdom of the dialogical process provides the context to differentiate truth from falsity.

5. Discerning experience means engaging the wisdom within experience itself, with particular attention to context and perspective. In this process of engagement we dialogue with each segment of experience, seeking to heed its internal messages, embracing new insight and learning, while all the while clarifying what is empowering rather than debilitating in our wider engagement with life at large.

6. As we trust experience and learn the skills to discern its deeper meaning, we empower ourselves, and others, to engage *the archetypal realm.* No matter how personal or individual an experience may seem, it evokes and awakens layers of meaning of a *transpersonal* nature, often connecting us to ancient myths and meaning systems we may not even be aware of at a conscious level.

7. The teacher (better seen as resource person) in the trans-formative learning experience is first and foremost a *facilitator* of shared wisdom. The primary wisdom will be that of the gathered group where the principle of the whole being greater than the sum of the parts is always at work. The potential wisdom and capacity for learning will be greater than any one individual, including the resource persons themselves.

8. *Dialogue,* therefore, is the core strategy in transformative learning. *Storytelling* is a foundational medium for exploration, and encountering new wisdom. In both storytelling and

dialogue, *listening* is the primary skill, without which creative learning will not take place.

9. *Spirituality* is inherently important for transformative learning. The agency for transformation is not located solely or even primarily in the person. It belongs to what indigenous peoples call the Great Spirit, the energetic-source that awakens potentiality at every level of creation, humanity included. In transformative learning, spirituality is deemed more foundational than religion and can be explored in its own right apart from formal belief systems.

10. As with all learning, the goal of the transformative approach is *integration,* except in this case the locus of such integration is not merely the individual person or group of people. Integration ensues in the creative dialogical interaction of Creation–the Spirit–the Person, all grounded in the planetary-cosmic context, the womb and wellspring from which everything evolves.

Edmund O'Sullivan et al. (2002) offer a valuable summary of transformative learning:

> Transformative learning involves experiencing a deep, structural shift in the basic premises of thought, feelings, and actions. It is a shift of consciousness that dramatically and permanently alters our way of being in the world. Such a shift involves our understanding of ourselves and our self-locations; our relationships with other humans and with the natural world; our understanding of relations of power in interlocking structures of class, race, and gender; our body-awarenesses, our visions of alternative approaches to living; and our sense of possibilities for social justice and peace and personal joy.

The Lure of the Future

Living in a world of mass information, we accumulate enormous reserves of practical knowledge. Much of this knowledge is useful, but a great deal of it is superficial and even downright destructive (as often exemplified via on-line information). And most of it is highly anthropomorphic, devised by people to serve people, as if people were the heart and soul of reality. The information needs to be supplemented with wisdom, with which we can perceive and understand more deeply and thus use our knowledge more creatively. In this way the accumulated wisdom can be put at the service of creation, not as a tool for manipulation and control, but to enhance a quality of mutual participation to the advantage of all living beings, the home planet included.

Faced as we are with the prospect of global warming, depleting resources, pollution, and human exploitation, it is becoming all too obvious that we need another way to engage the world and each other in our daily lives. In the words of the late Thomas Berry (2009, 118): "The issue has never been as critical as it is now. The human is at an impasse because we have brought the entire set of life systems of the planet to an impasse. The viability of the human is in question."

Humans are not behaving in a way that supports and enhances evolution's drive for complexity and new growth. Our inherited education, being essentially what Paulo Freire one time described as "education as domestication," has left us with numerous liabilities. We have been taught to be good patriarchal manipulators, to continue the game of divide and conquer, and compete as fiercely as possible with everything and everybody that challenges us. And we wonder why the world we inhabit has become such a violent place.

A growing body of humanity feels a lure to another way of being in the world. Our youth experience this quite intensely at times, but another lure quickly takes over with the prevailing emphasis on doing well at exams, to gain admittance into college, in order to get a good job, which will entitle them to plenty of money. Then this one-dimensional mode is likely to dominate their lives for many years — and does so for most people. As people mature in years — and this can be age thirty for some, age seventy for others — we find ourselves being drawn in another direction, urged to embrace a different way of living. This is what several contemporary writers call *the lure of the future*.[9]

Intuitively we know another way is possible, and we also know that it will take a major shift in consciousness to bring it about. It will take a revolution in our way of thinking rather than changes in our way of acting to inspire us to work for a different future. This awakening happens to people in a whole series of ways and means. It may begin with reading some recent book, attending a conference, or watching a TV documentary. After that we feel the lure, the challenge to get more deeply involved.

The Beleaguering Mix

In times of deep change, most people cling on to what feels safe and familiar. In fact, most people become entrenched in what they already know. And major institutions, consciously or unconsciously committed to self-perpetuation, also opt for the old familiar territory. The protean self is unlikely to find a congenial space within the realms of conventional living. To survive, the protean will veer to the liminal spaces where evolutionary awakening stands the best chance of flourishing.

Millions around the globe are likely to experience a sense of being trapped, restless, congested, and even alienated. In most cases, they will choose to do nothing about this dilemma, other than soften its impact through the various cultural escape routes so much taken for granted: alcohol consumption, drug relief (legal and illegal), gambling, hedonistic escapism, fundamentalist religiosity. The more intuitive are likely to opt for counseling or therapy. And those in denial and internally dominated by fear and insecurity are likely to invest more heavily in work, making money, playing power games, or acquiring further education to keep apace of the ever increasing cultural rat race.

For quite some time to come, the proteans are likely to remain a minority, and at times will appear to be disparate, chaotic, and even self-contradictory. And for many individuals it will be experienced as a lonely and frightening place, subject to misunderstanding, victimization, and rejection by old friends and even by one's own kin. In time the proteans will help to create one of evolution's critical thresholds — Rupert Sheldrake's morphic resonance (Sheldrake 2009) — with a likely breakthrough of greater clarity, an energy to organize (probably in networks), endowed with a clarity of perception and conviction that this is a more authentic way to honor the lure of the future.

As a species, we are not there yet, but there certainly is a growing momentum. And as the movement deepens so too will the resistance of major institutions. This is likely to be most notable among religious institutions with a tendency to demonize what is transpiring and scapegoat those fostering and encouraging it; instead the guardians of orthodoxy are likely to fall back on old devotional and even superstitious ways of behaving. Such reaction will create a semblance of security for those feeling threatened and vulnerable. This is the confused response endemic to times of major cultural change.

While noting this emergence and its transgressive disturbing nature, the primary purpose of the present book is to delineate likely scenarios of the unfolding future. These are already transpiring in an embryonic way. Many creative thinkers are piecing together elements of the emerging consciousness, e.g., the cultural creatives (Ray and Anderson 2000; *www.culturalcreatives.org)*. And the endeavor toward networking, the governance of the future, is probably much more advanced than many suspect. With this background context — and its foreground allurement — we will now look more closely at the ensuing spiritual developments likely to characterize the twenty-first century — and well beyond it.

(a) Conventional inherited wisdom views all learning as passed down from wiser seniors to inferior juniors, and learning is primarily obtaining the wherewithal to function effectively for the benefit of human society.

(b) Embedded codependency leaves children and adolescents feeling like passive absorbers in conventional learning settings, while adult aspiration and intelligence are grossly neglected and undermined.

(c) Adult empowerment perceives the adult as a full participant in a coeducational process where wisdom is owned by all and the teacher serves as a catalyst facilitating a transformative process of exploration and new discovery.

Chapter Nine

Toward a Spirituality of Homecoming

FOCUS: Because of a range of inherited ways of understanding life, we live far from ourselves and far from God. Now is a time for homecoming, and particularly to a quality of spiritual engagement befitting adult people serving an adult God.

Consider what you mean when you tell someone: be realistic. It's another way to say: lower your expectations. It's also connected with a view of maturity that holds growing up to be a process of becoming resigned. — Susan Neiman

A LL EVOLUTION is about growth and development, frequently including radically new features. Yet evolution is never entirely new, and in each wave it brings with it the cumulative achievements of former times. This is sometimes called the process of recapitulation.

Cultural developments of the 1960s highlight this process. Huge numbers of young people adopted modes of dress and behavior that, on the surface, suggested a regression into a more tribalistic, primitive past: unkempt dress, exaggerated body deportment, sexual freedom, rejection of city life styles, return to nature, etc. There was a tendency then, and there still is, to judge by external behaviors as if these were deliberate conscious choices.

In the process of cultural recapitulation, subconscious drives far outpace conscious choices. Subsections of the human species, in this case young people, were serving as catalysts for the entire body, seeking to reclaim ancient wisdom (exemplified in certain external behaviors) in order to be better endowed for the evolutionary shift forward. Subconsciously they were opting for the future rather than regressing into the past.

The Spiritual Cosmopolitan

Similarly in our time, the coevolutionary protean adult faces what seems like unprecedented challenges, but in truth we have been there before. In fact, we have frequently been there throughout our long evolutionary history. This new desire for another way of being adult is not entirely innovative or avant-garde; the evolutionary context in which it is unfolding is new and demands of all of us radically novel options in how we might respond. This is where spirituality becomes very central to our evolutionary unfolding at this time.

Similarly, spirituality is seen not as a peripheral issue but as a core element in the process of transformative learning. Authentic adult development, even intellectually, requires a grounding in that expansive wisdom that enables us to make sense of the larger picture. That is a central feature of spirituality as we understand it afresh today.

This enlarged horizon of spiritual engagement can be explored in a number of different ways. As an entry point, I wish to incorporate the seminal insights from a landmark book by the American feminist theologians, Rita Nakashima Brock and Rebecca Parker (2008), documenting a spiritual ambivalence that has dogged Christianity for well over one thousand years. Our relationship with God's creation has been riddled with ambiguity. While consistently asserting the fundamental goodness of everything God has created, Christians were encouraged to flee the world, abandon the world, turn their back on the world, and look forward to the day when they could escape from this vale of tears to obtain everlasting peace in their heavenly home — *outside and beyond this flawed creation.*

This left many humans bewildered and unsure about their grounding in the real world and their adult place within it. It gave way to a kind of cultural passivity and codependency that still fuels adherence in many of the great religions. In extreme cases, it leads to human and spiritual infantilism.

Particularly throughout the second millennium, words like "exile," "alienation," and "estrangement" populated the popular spiritual literature. The central message was: humans are not meant to feel at home in this world. God is not to be encountered here, but in the hereafter. The spiritual life involves a long struggle to stay on the straight and narrow, so that we win redemption in the end. And in this highly convoluted schema, adult wisdom is not invoked: even as adults we are essentially sinful, wayward children, totally at the mercy of the demanding patriarchal God.

Some contemporary scholars will try to counter this exaggerated outline. Others, while acknowledging its essential truth, suggest we simply regard it as a set of perceptions that belongs to another time, which we should now leave to rest in the past and move forward in a more holistic way. Brock and Parker (2008) present a very different analysis, a comprehensive and critical examination of key Christian symbols whose core meaning needs to be reevaluated and reappropriated in order to embrace a more adult sense of faith for contemporary times.

The Rise of Violent Spirituality

Throughout the first Christian millennium, Christian spirituality often embraced the notion of paradise. On a more careful reading of key texts and sources related to this prolonged time-span, paradise denotes a lifestyle striving to bring about love and justice on this earth and not an escapist spirituality seeking a state of happiness in a world beyond. Paradise was a here-and-now experiential domain, an attempt, however imperfect, to realize the Kingdom of God on earth and not a utopian existence in a life hereafter.[10]

Brock and Parker (2008) suggest that this present-world focus continued until the Middle Ages and began to change as the Christian understanding of Christ's death assumed primary significance in Christian spirituality. A central icon of this new understanding was the emaciated and tortured Christ on the cross, congruent with much of the Atonement thinking of the twelfth and thirteenth centuries and formally endorsed by Pope Urban II in 1095, when he admonished those going to fight in the Christian Crusades to wear visible images of the crucified Jesus as a validation for the task they were undertaking. From there on the word "paradise" took on a different meaning: salvation in a life hereafter obtained through union with the suffering Christ on the cross. Salvation in paradise came to be associated with escape through death to a life beyond, rather than the previous understanding, for which the primary focus was the spiritual renewal of life, in and with the created order.[11]

From the thirteenth century on, Christian spirituality took a new direction, a fact that does not seem to have been acknowledged by many scholars ancient and modern. True fulfillment, human and spiritual, belonged to the afterlife, not this life. The acquisition of this final destiny could be achieved only by internalizing — in disposition and action — the sufferings of the crucified Christ. The more intense those sufferings and the more willingly embraced, the greater would be the reward hereafter.

People aspiring to a more adult appropriation of faith simply cannot accept what they perceive to be a rather deranged paradigm. They abhor the violence endemic to such a spirituality; suffering for the sake of suffering cannot be regarded as a spiritual ideal in a world already overwhelmed by so much meaningless suffering. And the historical tendency to either demand or to impose suffering as a requirement for holiness is seen as a foundation for ecclesiastical abuse that has prevailed over many centuries.

The underlying phenomenology of both person and planet also requires radical reexamination. Is the spurious notion of original sin the corrupting influence in the entire approach? If creation came into being and is sustained by the power and creativity of God, how could it be fundamentally flawed? If humans essentially reflect the divine imprint why begin with a sense of original curse rather than with the grace of original blessing? Certain foundational assumptions seem to have outlived their usefulness and indeed may have been culturally conditioned — and spiritually defective — from the very beginning. They violate more foundational truths emerging in our time and of particular significance for adult faith in the twenty-first century.

The inherited, conventional spirituality heavily emphasized our true home in heaven. Therefore any sense of being at home in this world, or seeing creation as a special presence of the Holy One, was deemed not merely inappropriate, but downrightly heretical. Three metaphors dominated the spiritual literature:

1. *Exile:* With the adoption of a rather literal interpretation of the Jewish people in exile — whether in Babylon or Egypt — it is suggested that humans are essentially creatures in exile, far from God and from the happiness that only life with God in heaven can procure. Therefore, the earth is a place of exile, and even more so the cosmos at large. Heaven, as the domain of everlasting fulfillment, is considered to be above and outside the created universe.

2. *Alienation:* Since humans are prone to sin, born with the stain of original sin, they can never hope to be able to live harmoniously with God, nor with each other. Things are essentially out of kilter — because of original sin. And according to the long tradition of spiritual wisdom, it appears that while humans are on earth, there will always be a sense of alienation from God and from our true selves.

3. *Estrangement:* This is the ensuing condition arising from the sense of exile and alienation referred to above. Here — in this vale of tears — we don't have a lasting city. Meaningless pain and suffering are our lot, and there is not a great deal we can do about it. It very much sounds like we are victims of a rather capricious deity, holding a lot of grudges. And the adult rightly asks: Who invented the deity in the first place?

Indeed, the God portrayed in this state of spiritual estrangement violates even our inherited Christian tradition — one we share with all the major religions — namely, that the God we believe in is a God of unconditional love. This God of ours loves, without any conditions. In a sense it does not matter how depraved we are or how reckless we become, God still loves us unconditionally. How can anyone be alienated, exiled, or estranged from one who shows unconditional love? Impossible, it seems to me.

The person of adult faith quickly intuits that God is not the problem, but rather a set of distorted human perceptions, enculturated in deviant religiosity. We are not, and never could be — alienated from a God of unconditional love. Our sense of alienation, which is real, has nothing to do with God; instead it has everything to do with God's creation. We are alienated, disconnected, from the web of life to which we intimately belong. In the words of Thomas Berry (2009, 94), "Our alienation from earth is one of the most significant causes of our alienation from each other."

In this regard we fare worse than our ancient ancestors, who for much of their time were intimately embedded in the living web of creation, and as I frequently stated in a previous work (O'Murchu 2008), *we got it right most of the time.* Because we got it right, we did not experience the alienation and estrangement so endemic to our modern way of living.

The problem, therefore, is not that we are a godless generation so much as we are a *disembodied species.* We are not at home on the earth, the primary body that nourishes and sustains us. In some cases, religion itself has pitted humans against the created universe, maligned as a sinful place, a distraction from living an authentic spiritual life, and therefore a realm from which we should seek escape rather than any kind of meaningful engagement.

Contemporary environmentalists often allude to the destruction humans exert on the living earth. Much more serious is the destruction we have wrought upon ourselves as creatures of the earth. The earth will survive our waywardness, but it looks increasingly dubious if we will survive ourselves. Indeed, our self-destruction may be necessary for the earth, and its other inhabitants, to continue to grow and thrive in the evolutionary web of life.

A New Spiritual Metaphor: Homecoming

We need to abandon the tedious rhetoric of alienation and estrangement. We need to outgrow the cultural and religious victimization.

We need to transcend the pseudo-spiritual games of "divine abandonment." We need to reclaim our *adult* place in an *adult* relationship with an *adult* God, modeled eminently for us by the *adult* Jesus. We need to come home to a new way of being and seeing and doing. For people of adult faith, *homecoming* is the great spiritual challenge of our time.

Homecoming needs to become the new spiritual metaphor for the twenty-first century. The well-worn metaphors of *exile, alienation* and *estrangement* no longer serve us in a responsible or empowering way. They feed our spiritual narcissism instead of enabling us to resolve it. We need to outgrow our dysfunctional dependence on a rescuing God. Such a God is a projection of our entrenchment in a cult of perpetual childishness. In the face of this we also have invented a divine superhero, who paradoxically is both heroic and childish. Some regard him in absolute subservience, while others denounce him in absolute abhorrence.

The homecoming embraces a range of different dimensions. It is not so much what we do as what we allow to embrace us. The first level of engagement is that of the cosmic landscape where God first encounters our creation in the dynamic of unhindered creativity.

Gordon Lynch (2007) argues that we are witnessing the rise of a new religious counterculture that reveres the natural world, connects religious faith with novel scientific theories, and has a forward-looking agenda for society's transformation. These three elements provide useful guidelines for an empowering adult spirituality for the future.

Adult Spirituality

First, a few observations on spirituality itself. In recent decades spirituality has been breaking loose from mainline religion. Various contemporary theorists have noted this development: Heelas (2008), King (2009), Lynch (2007), O'Murchu (1998), Tacey (2004). Churches, and mainline religions, seem very much in denial about this emerging phenomenon, leaving adult seekers often unsure where to turn for support and encouragement in their discerning search.

The following are some of the key features of spirituality in the twenty-first century, with an obvious appeal for those seeking more adult ways to engage and articulate their faith.

- Spirituality is the human response to what many indigenous cultures call the Great Spirit, the primary embodiment of Holy Mystery throughout the entire web of life. This creative life force is perceived to be transpersonal (embracing human personhood but more importantly incorporating everything else in creation often derogatorily labeled as impersonal).

- Spirituality seeks to explore and understand how the Great Spirit infuses and animates the energy that enlivens and sustains everything in creation. To engage this wisdom, we need a multidisciplinary strategy, with modern science and cosmology providing significant insights.

- Spirituality cherishes *relationality* (relationship) as the primary dynamic through which everything in creation — people included — is sustained and flourishes. This relational dynamic seems to be reflected in all the great religions — via one or other rendering of the Christian notion of the Trinity.

- Spirituality seeks truth through dialogical discernment of lived experience rather than relying on dogmas, religious or scientific. It views the scriptures as culturally conditioned guides to orthopraxy rather than unchangeable repositories of unalterable truths.

- Spirituality highlights the call to transformative living, enculturating the earth's own wisdom to guide our moral and personal choices in our commitment to contemplation (seeing rightly) and to justice-making (acting rightly). Spirituality acknowledges the need for structures (not necessarily major institutions), which need to be kept supple and creative with a strong sense of mutual accountability.

- Spirituality seeks to honor creation's core paradox of birth–death–rebirth, which it views not as a flaw, but as a paradox necessary for the creative freedom and flourishing of all the creatures who inhabit planet earth (see chapter 11).

+ Spirituality denounces all forms of anthropocentrism, considering humans as unique and integral to God's creation but with no right to mastery or patriarchal control, a form of domination that it considers to be the primary cause of so much meaningless suffering in the world.

+ Some commentators cite the maintenance and fostering of *human rights* as a key ingredient of the new spirituality. I suggest that all rights — and not merely human ones — need to be included. On the human level, I find the notion of *capabilities,* as developed by Martha Nussbaum (2001; 2007), much more congenial to the spirit of the emerging spirituality.

+ Some authors (e.g., Carrette and King [2005] and Heelas [2008]) highlight the shadow elements — false romanticism, consumerism, self-inflation — that also characterize the new spirituality. I suspect these deviations are not as widespread as these critics suggest and where they do prevail, they need to be subjected to a much deeper analysis than is usually provided.

Using these observations as a backdrop, we can revisit Lynch's three features of our spiritual emergence at the present time:

1. *Reverence for the natural world.* Creation is the first and oldest revelation of God to and for us humans. God was at work in creation for billions of years before humans ever evolved or before religions of churches ever came to be. Creation will always remain God's primary paradise. It is not an object to be conquered or controlled, but a living organism without which our lives have no meaning. It is the origin of our spiritual awareness, the context of our spiritual engagement, and the wellspring of every blessing that comes our way. Our political and economic exploitation of the earth, our scientific tendency to objectify it, and our religious dismissive dualisms are all based on a destructive patriarchal ideology, rapidly losing credibility for adult people striving to live more authentically in today's turbulent world.

2. *Linking faith with novel scientific theories.* Formal religions exhibit a tendency to divide all reality into opposing dualisms: the sacred vs. the secular. Integration of commonalities rather than

splitting based on differences is a foundational desire of the new spirituality. The scientific insights of strongest appeal are those that facilitate openness to further discovery and understanding rather than those that seek closed and definitive ways of thinking or being. Quantum cosmology, with its indeterminacy and open possibilities, is a favored choice with strong links detected with the great mystical traditions of humanity.

3. *A forward-looking agenda for society's transformation.* Religion seeks truth in the certainties of the past, and in some fundamentalist contexts, it clings to the past with a kind of literal, legalistic allegiance. The emerging spirituality seeks to build on the past but always reinterpreting the inherited wisdom in terms of new insight (coming from multidisciplinary awareness), seeking solutions to the pressing problems that keep humanity and the suffering earth in bondage to unnecessary pain and trauma due to exploitation and manipulation. In this endeavor, hope, rather than faith or love, is the primary target, seeking to counter the despair to which many of the planet's creatures are subjected on an almost permanent basis.

Spiritual homecoming is the hunger of our age. Something from deep within tells us we should be able feel at home on this earth. Escape to a promised land beyond this creation does not have the appeal of former times. Intuitively, more and more people suspect that the afterlife is a dimension of this life; our dead are all around us as cosmic creatures living at other vibrational levels. In the power of the Great Spirit, everything belongs to the one web of life. In our fragmented, conflictual, and competitively driven conditioning we are alienated from our true selves.

Normalcy has thrown us into exile. Our normal way of living is full of lies. More and more people intuit that things are not right, and it is up to us — responsible adults — to sort out our inherited cultural mess. There is no God figure in the sky or elsewhere who will do it for us. The Great Spirit, who is radically present within and among us, has blessed us, and continues to bless us, with all the resources we need. And from a Christian perspective, Jesus offers us a model of how it can be done. Let's get on with the task!

(a) **Conventional inherited wisdom** is dictated by the claim that
we are people in exile, alienated and estranged from God, from
each other, and from creation. The only place where we can
hope to feel at home is in heaven, outside and beyond this vale
of tears.

(b) **Embedded codependency** traps us in slavery to a capricious
God, represented on earth by those who want to keep us as
childishly dependent as possible.

(c) **Adult empowerment** means reclaiming our rightful place at
home in God's creation, through which we are endowed with
everything we need to grow and flourish as God desires for us.

Chapter Ten

Stages in Adult Faith Development

FOCUS: In the past, passing on the faith was done with emphasis on doctrines and morality, failing to distinguish adult appropriation from that of the child. Today, people are discovering spiritual meaning and insight either through personal search or through mutual exploration, birthing a fresh sense of adult faith and seeking new understandings of how faith is appropriated in an adult way.

We are getting used to the idea that adulthood is not static. We are coming to terms with the insight that change is normative, continuous, and consequential. — JAMES FOWLER

The prison where we sleep away our lives becomes visible only in and through the experience of stepping out.
— DOROTHEE SOELLE

THE HOMECOMING EXPLORED in the last chapter involves among other things the reexamination of the spiritual foundations of our daily existence. We cannot live meaningfully without a meaningful spirituality, which translates into connecting more creatively with the spiritual foundations that underpin not merely human existence but indeed the entire fabric of creation at large. This enlarged context of spiritual meaning is a relatively new phenomenon and as yet poorly integrated into how we live our faith in the realm of formal religion.

This expansive vision still feels strange to many people. Yet deep within it is precisely what millions are hungering for. Many people are weary of the suffocating impact of popular religiosity, the paternalizing promises of a far-fetched utopia that feels more unreal by the day. It smacks of a childish codependency that increasing numbers of adults seek to outgrow. In a word, millions are seeking a more adult way to live their faith as adults.

From the Child to the Adult

In developmental psychology, the attainment of adulthood tends to be taken for granted. The focus of attention is very much on that of children growing through formative tender years, with the widespread belief that the foundations laid in childhood will impact upon our well-being for the rest of our lives. For much of the twentieth century, psychologists assumed that character was formed by late adolescence and remained largely unchanged for the rest of the human lifespan.

Similarly with passing on the faith. In all the world religions, transmission of faith is deemed to be crucial during the young and formative years, the assumption being that what is imparted at this early stage will stand the test of time throughout the rest of one's life. Despite extensive evidence to the contrary, passing on the faith to youth is still considered to be significant for the adult appropriation of faith. In the past this has often resulted in serious neglect of how adults appropriate faith in their adult years. That is the material being explored in the present chapter.

In terms of educational strategy, it is widely assumed that what works for the child will work for the adult. Even in universities around the world, information is still imparted in a condescending manner, with the resource person (the teacher) holding the monopoly of wisdom and the student participating mainly as a passive recipient. In 1987, the National Center for Research in Vocational Education at Ohio State University (Columbus) drew up a program highlighting some of the different learning strategies appropriate for children and adults. The differences are significant, as seen in the table on the following page.

There are notable differences in the two approaches. Adults bring to the learning context a range of experiences that instinctively and intuitively they integrate into the learning context. Adults learn best

DIFFERING LEARNING STRATEGIES

Childhood	*Adulthood*
Children depend upon adults for material support, psychological support, and life management. They are other-directed.	Adults depend upon themselves for material support and life management. Although they must still meet many psychological needs through others, they are largely self-directed.
Children perceive one of their major roles in life to be that of learner.	Adults perceive themselves to be doers; using previous learning to achieve success as workers, parents, etc.
Children, to a large degree, learn what they are told to learn.	Adults learn best when they perceive the outcomes of the learning process as valuable — contributing to their own development, work success, etc.
Children view the established learning content as important because adults tell them it is important.	Adults often have very different ideas about what is important to learn.
Children, as a group within educational settings, are much alike. They're approximately the same age, come from similar socioeconomic backgrounds, etc.	Adults are very different from each other. Adult learning groups are likely to be composed of persons of many different ages, cultural backgrounds, education levels, various life experiences, etc.
Children actually perceive time differently than older people do. Our perception of time changes as we age — time seems to pass more quickly as we get older.	Adults, in addition to perceiving time itself differently than children do, are more concerned about the effective use of time.
Children have a limited experience base.	Adults have a broad, rich experience base to which to relate new learning.
Children generally learn quickly.	Adults, for the most part, learn more slowly than children, but they internalize and integrate information more deeply.
Children are open to new information and will readily adjust their views.	Adults are much more likely to evaluate the pros and cons of new learning.
Children's readiness to learn is linked to both academic development and biological development.	Adults' readiness to learn is more directly linked to need — needs related to fulfilling their roles as workers, spouses, parents, etc. and coping with life changes (divorce, death of a loved one, retirement, etc.).
Children learn (at least in part) because learning will be of use in the future.	Adults are more concerned about the immediate applicability of learning.
Children are often externally motivated (by the promise of good grades, praise from teachers and parents, etc.).	Adults are more often internally motivated (by the potential for feelings of worth, self-esteem, achievement, etc.).
Children have less well formed sets of expectations in terms of formal learning experiences. Their "filter" of past experience is smaller than that of adults.	Adults have well-formed expectations, which, unfortunately, are sometimes negative because they are based upon unpleasant past formal learning experiences.

through dialogue and mutual exchange. And they want the new learnings to be practical and capable of being integrated into their life experience. The adult thrives when the teacher becomes a fellow-adult in a mutual exploration of shared wisdom. Mutuality and participation are central to adult learning.

Applying these principles to faith education is a formidable challenge. When it comes to faith formation, it is still widely assumed that what works for the child will work for the adult. We ensure that our children (and adolescents) get a solid grasp of the faith, an awareness of the key doctrines and practices, which, hopefully, they will retain for the rest of their lives. Faith is understood as a gift from God appropriated through commitment to a specific set of beliefs, encapsulated in ethics, doctrine, and worship. Basically, you either have it or you don't. And the foundational elements never change!

According to this conventional paradigm, strictly speaking, there is no such thing as adult faith development. What we believe in, and practice, as adults is merely a continuation of what we learned as children or as adolescents. One of the disturbing consequences of this approach is that parents often fob off their offspring with pet catechetical answers they learned twenty or forty years previously, beliefs they still hold, blindly rather than reflectively, that may not speak very intelligibly to a younger generation seeking more reflective answers.

In the contemporary world of mass information, understandings change consistently. In most intellectual disciplines, updating and retraining have become not merely normal practice, but in many situations are now obligatory. In the public perception, however, religion and the appropriation of faith do not yet seem to have caught up with this new hermeneutical moment. Lifelong learning, rather than a one time only acquisition of key knowledge, has become the guiding criterion of this time.

Adult Faith Development

Developmental psychologist James Fowler recognized this shift in the 1970s and set forth a daring and visionary reconstruction of how humans appropriate faith amid the cultural complexities and information explosion of our time. The originality and authenticity of Fowler's insights are widely recognized despite a limited research base of 359 people, all white, and mainly of the Judaeo-Christian tradition. Fowler bases his research on the theoretical foundations laid by Erik Erikson (developmental life stages), Daniel J. Levinson (seasons and transitions), Robert Kegan (organizational skills), Jean Piaget (intellectual development), Robert L. Selman (the construction of social perspective), and Lawrence Kohlberg (moral development). Fowler's work has been extensively reviewed. Its original elements have been endorsed and some of its limitations highlighted. Francis and Astley (1992) provide a comprehensive and critical overview.

One of the oft-cited weaknesses of Fowler's work is his "inbuilt andocentric bias" (Slee 2004, 9) and his lack of a cross-cultural basis. Nicola Slee (2004) provides a comprehensive analysis of women's faith development, indicating that the process is more relational and nonlinear than Fowler suggests. Quoting A. S. Ostriker, she writes:

> Unlike the epic hero, however, the female protagonist does not know her own goal in advance and must discover it through fluid adventure — meditation, memory, prayer, questioning, and associative weavings. And unlike the epic hero, her role is not to support but unravel and rewrite the already-written drama or script of religion and history. (Slee 2004, 98)

Beverley Lanzetta (2005) endorses these complementary values in her analysis of female mysticism, indicating once again the central role of relationality, transpersonal as well as personal, and emphasizing the primacy of process over outcomes characterized by specific expectations. In this overview, the research of Martha Nussbaum (2001) on key capabilities is also noteworthy. These additional insights apply not merely to gender differences but alert us to complexities arising from cultural, ethnic, and historical features as well.

Notwithstanding the limitations highlighted in these critiques, all acknowledge the original and creative wisdom inherent in Fowler's seminal research. His most controversial claims include a call to honor *adolescence as a time for questioning and rebellion,* not a moment for the appropriation of a mature faith. That an eighteen-year-old person could internalize a mature sense of faith is unacceptable to Fowler. Such ownership and understanding of faith are not likely to happen until people are well into their twenties, and for many it may not happen until they begin to negotiate a midlife transition experience (sometime between thirty-five and fifty-five).

Several years previously, psychologist Carl G. Jung had suggested that the appropriation of genuine adult faith very much belonged to the midlife stage, often consequential on a psychological breakdown of one type or another. To embrace the new, a shedding of the old had to take place, and that frequently seemed to require a life crisis, leading to a more reflective review of life's meaning itself.

Fowler is also very revolutionary in proposing the declining years of life (60+) as potentially a deeply reflective time open to new cosmic vision and the appropriation of a more global sense of spirituality. Susan Cook-Greuter (1994; 1999) endorses this insight in what she describes as the postautonomous stage. It is characterized by two phases: first *the construct aware phase* in which people review more critically their inherited linguistic and metaphorical concepts, and *the unitive phase* experienced as a transcendence of the subject-object polarity along with a deepening sense of being at one with everything in creation.

The unitive's worldview is universal and cosmic. Persons experiencing this stage of development can see themselves as part of the ongoing flow of humanity. They hold the personal and universal together without a sense of opposition and can embrace paradox, inconsistency, and ambiguity with relative ease. They view the vast array of human experience and history from the witness perspective and can respect and value differences while maintaining integrity. Unitives care deeply about the human condition and from an internalized moral position can respond with justice on behalf of the whole. Without elaborate ego defenses, unitives are nonattached to outcomes and nonjudgmental toward others. Cook-Greuter claims that only 20 percent of American adults consciously reach this stage of developmental and spiritual growth. The majority remain stuck —

and often happily so — at levels of understanding that often have changed little since their early years.

This is a highly countercultural claim in a world that regards the elderly as a financial burden and an economic/social liability. In some industrialized countries people over the age of fifty find it impossible to obtain paid employment, leaving many with the painful experience that they are no longer "useful" and therefore can be left with the feeling of being abandoned into a kind of brutal cultural wasteland.

The American psychologist and ecotherapist Bill Plotkin (2008) also adopts a stages approach in his analysis of what he calls "modern soul-craft" (see online *www.natureandthehumansoul.com/newbook/aboutBill.htm*). Situating the search for spiritual meaning in the context of the cosmic and planetary consciousness of modern cosmology and science, Plotkin moves beyond the anthropocentric focus of Fowler (and those who have inspired him), to an enlarged vision with greater potential for developmental integration.

Plotkin delineates two phases of childhood (the *Innocent* and the *Explorer*) and a further two phases for adolescence (*Peer Influence* and the *Wanderer*). He describes the task of the early adult years as that of learning delivery systems for embodying soul in culture and highlights innovation as an outstanding feature of midlife. Like Cook-Greuter, he also divides the older years into two stages, with a progressive deepening of a planetary and cosmic consciousness.

For the adult years he depicts a gradual transcending of the functional roles of wage earner and home-provider in favor of a more-than-human engagement with the cultural and spiritual challenges of being cosmic earthlings. This reclaiming of our earthiness is suggested to be the basis of that deeper integration through which we realize more fully our calling to be adult people of faith, serving the adult God, inviting us into *a deeper communion with everything in the cosmic web of life.*

The Journey of Faith

In the outline below, I adopt Fowler's schema but expand his outline to include other emerging insights of our time — particularly those of Susan Cook-Greuter and Bill Plotkin. Along with Fowler I follow many of the well-known developmental theorists outlining the dynamics for childhood and adolescence. My primary interest is that of postadolescent faith development. Adult faith development has been the neglected element that now needs serious attention. It is largely ignored by churches and by institutions dealing with religious formation. For most people, our engagement with faith, and with life generally, happens in the adult phase from our early twenties right through to our eighties. In educational terms it is irresponsible and unjust to neglect this challenge.

The Former Paradigm: Faith is a set of defined dogmas, passed on from "seniors" to "juniors" and lived out primarily (if not exclusively) in the context of the church.

The Organic Paradigm: Faith is a gift but one of cocreative significance, which we appropriate and articulate in accordance with various life stages, attending in a more informed way to the growth and development that characterize those stages.

Stage 1: *Primal Faith (ages 0–2)*: Security, trust and love are the key qualities for these early years. Experiential appropriation of religious sentiment by the newborn infant tends to be largely subconscious.

Stage 2: *Intuitive-projective (ages 2–6)*: Impressionistic world of early childhood, largely human-centered, often accompanied by strong emotion (tantrums). Appropriate stimulation seems to be important at this stage.

Stage 3: *Mythic-literal (ages 6–12)*: First conscious appropriation of an inherited faith tradition; Plotkin's stage of the explorer in the garden. Saving childhood and keeping "adulthood" at bay is a challenge for this phase.

The integration of these first three stages is a lifelong challenge, particularly regarding the "inner child" as a crucial dimension of a fulfilled adult existence.

Stage 4: *Synthetic-conventional (ages 12–20)*: Puberty and through adolescence, a love-hate appropriation, with a tendency toward rebellion. Honoring the rebel is the big challenge here, while resisting the cultural expectation of attaining religious maturity by the late teenage years.

Stage 5: *Individuative-reflective (ages 20–35)*: Engaging with cultural expectations regarding work, relationships, and civic commitments, rejection of religion is also a likely outcome. Questions of meaning tend to be suspended or suppressed, and when entertained the search for a meaningful "spirituality" may begin to surface. Males tend to opt out; females explore alternatives.

Stage 6: *Conjunctive (i.e., balanced, inclusive:)* Midlife stage *(ages 35–55)*: A time of transition, paradox, and letting-go, but also one that can be characterized by a strong urge for innovation (Ploktin). For females, menopause may provide the catalyst for a significant spiritual adjustment. Males are more likely to revert to a second adolescence. Both sexes may begin to embark upon a search for more mature faith, sometimes requiring a change of church or religion.

Stage 7: *Coming home time (ages 55–70)*: Acknowledgment of declining years with three possible religious outcomes: return to a conventional practice; reclaiming agnostic (atheistic) stance (often privately); embracing a more universal sense of spiritual awakening. Plotkin describes this stage as that of the Master in the grove of Elders, a time for new adjustments, with a degree of uncertainty on how best to do this.

Stage 8: *Universalizing faith (ages 70+)*: Described by Plotkin as the sage in the mountain cave. Two tendencies have been noted: (a) Fearful at the imminent prospect of "meeting God" in death and consequently opting for the safe, conventional approach to faith; (b) Altruistic, love-embracing option for life; a deep sense of gratitude whatever the circumstances. The latter is more widespread than we think, rarely recognized and one of the most serious areas of pastoral and developmental neglect.

These insights are *not* widely adopted in education generally or in religious formation specifically. Childhood education is much better informed with this wisdom than other spheres. As indicated in the last chapter, attention to the developmental wisdom of the adult is central to the process of transformative learning, and even some university programs promote this approach. However, amid the adult population it is little more than the proverbial drop in the bucket.

For faith development, I suggest four areas that need extensive and immediate attention:

1. Growth in faith is a developmental process happening throughout an entire lifespan with the most significant learning and integration taking place during the adult years. Faith as a developmental process belongs first and foremost to the adult stages and not merely to younger years.

2. Faith is not merely an inherited set of intellectual or religious truths based simply on Holy Writ or an inherited religious tradition. Faith is a psychic capacity (a soul craft), an innate endowment of every person. Many people are not even aware of this capacity, and millions have not been formed or skilled on how best to mobilize this empowering potential.

3. When authentic faith development is neglected, the human spirit will seek out compensatory satisfactions, and these can easily become compulsive or addictive. Formal religions can easily feed those addictions, as we see in a range of contemporary religious ideologies, some heavily committed to power (fundamentalists), others to violence (e.g., suicide bombers), and others to consumerist spirituality (see Carrette and King 2005; Heelas 2008).

4. Wise elders play an important role in various indigenous faith traditions, and the emergence in our time of more older people embracing Fowler's universalizing stage has substantial cultural and spiritual implications for the future of human civilization. We know the world population is growing older with a promise of future hope that only a few researchers have noted (see Roszak 2001). Our youth also lack inspiring adult models — at several levels. Cultivating wise elders needs to become an integral dimension of adult catechesis for the future.

When Adults Do Theology

When adults engage with their faith in a more conscious and informed way, they are automatically entering the realm of theological discernment. They ask questions of deeper meaning and seek out those deeper truths we formally describe as *theology*. Since about the mid-twentieth century (after 1950), Christian theology began to abandon the ecclesiastical enclave. Nobody drove it away from there. It left freely and almost unobtrusively. However, that departure marks a breakthrough that could create theological global tremors throughout the course of the twenty-first century.

As already indicated in Part One, lay people do theology very differently from priests. The latter, consciously or otherwise, prioritize the church, its traditions, teachings, and expectations. Lay theologians seem much more concerned about the theological questions arising from engagement with the surrounding world. The gross exploitation of the earth and its resources, national and tribal rivalries, religious conflict, poverty, globalization (positively and negatively), the fragmentation of major institutions, access to global information, the power of networking, religious pluralism — these and many other issues that press on us provide the raw material for adult lay theological discernment.

Transcending the old distinction between the sacred and the secular, this new generation of theologians is asking a different set of questions, giving birth to daring new theological horizons (see Vigil et al. 2010). These questions include: How do we encounter and serve the living God, not in some distant heaven, but right in our midst as cosmic, planetary beings? How do we discern and respond to the new awakenings the Spirit of God makes possible in our time? What are the new prophetic thresholds to which people of faith are being called? How do we translate living faith into structures that empower justice and liberation for the millions condemned to poverty and oppression? How do we cultivate a spirituality (or religion) that can transcend the addiction to patriarchal power? How do we develop and promote a spiritual (and religious) praxis that will mobilize adult participation in an empowering and liberating way?

The shift from dogmatic answers to discerning questions creates the context for a new theological ferment: interpersonal, ecumenical, multifaith, ecological, and cross-cultural. There are no experts in this field and there is no definitive revelation, other than the unfolding challenge we encounter every day at the heart of a cosmic and planetary creation where the creative divine Spirit never ceases to invigorate and sustain the complex mystery within which we are all held and within which everything is empowered to flourish. And, as all the religions indicate (in one form or another), it is a Trinitarian relational God, cocreating the web of life in the empowering animation of the Great Spirit. This is fertile territory for adult faith, and the relational context in which it can thrive and flourish is the subject of our next chapter.

(a) *Conventional inherited wisdom regards faith as a set of beliefs passed on from wise seniors to the uninitiated, who should be able to grasp the truth of faith by the end of the adolescent stage of development.*

(b) *Embedded codependency keeps many adults trapped in an understanding and appropriation of faith that never matured beyond the adolescent stage of learning.*

(c) *Adult empowerment sees faith as a divine gift that grows, matures, and develops in accordance with developmental life stages. Faith formation is an open, lifelong process, with the potential — in old age — of blossoming into a sense of universal wholeness, provided previous stages have been negotiated in a good enough way.*

Chapter Eleven

Expanding Cultural Horizons

FOCUS: Our inherited spirituality distrusts the material creation; our inherited politics and economics commodifies creation. As people called to adult discipleship we need to revision afresh how we relate to God's creation.

> *Rather than rebellion against God being the primary sin that engenders all others, I see rebellion against creation as the fundamental sin.* — Marjorie Suchocki

> *A true adult is someone who understands why (s)he is here on earth, why (s)he was born, and is offering a unique contribution to the more-than-human world.* — Bill Plotkin

WE LIVE IN THE MIDST of creation. Each day we breathe its air, consume its nutrients, and if time permits admire its beauty. Most people take creation for granted: it is part of the landscape within which our existence unfolds. More importantly, it is there for *our* use and benefit. It is an object we manage, hopefully in a way that will procure our happiness and progress.

And after all that, we hope we will receive due reward in *another* world! In fact, most people are so preoccupied in getting the best out of life here on earth, they rarely worry about an afterlife. For long, the religions tried to convince us that we lived in a vale of tears, an alien condition from which we would escape through the portal of death; and millions took the religions at their word. But not anymore! Scepticism and functionality now rule the roost; make the best of it while you are here, because this is probably all there is!

Most people seem to collude with the objectification and commodification of the earth and its resources and seem totally unaware of the ensuing sense of alienation. Others, those evolving along the adult lines explored in previous chapters, tend to be more aware of humanity's place in the living world and how we might play more creative roles. To date, this is largely a development among retired, white Westerners (mainly in the United States), but as the "New Story" burrows its way into the changing consciousness of our time people begin to resonate with its empowering vision. This relatively new awakening — with its cosmic and planetary implications — impacts significantly on the expanded sense of adulthood being explored in this book.

Bruce Wilshire (1998, 38, 39), claims that the rise in addictive behaviors today is a confused reaction to our growing alienation as we become ever more separated from the cosmic web of life and the natural world in which we are embedded:

> Disconnection from nature in the name, ironically, of natural science leaves a bottomless pit. Addictive behaviors pour into it.... Without an all-inclusive ritual matrix in which human development is keyed to participation in nature's cycles, things tend to fall apart.

And for many they do fall apart, but not for all. Ironically, alienation can also beget its very opposite, namely, fresh hope and optimism. It appears that humans won't tolerate a dysfunctional cosmology for too long. Something deep within tells us that we really do belong here and should see this as our goal and the inspiration for our life's work. In fact, millions are reclaiming a fresh sense of earthly belonging and cosmic contextualization. Even rational science is embracing the breakthrough.

Our Primal Belonging

In my human and Christian upbringing, the benchmark of two thousand years was presented as the nodal point around which everything in life evolved. That date marked the moment of God's supreme intervention in the person of Jesus. From there on "salvation" had a grip on reality; prior to that time, sin and paganism were the prevailing forces. In fact, the significance of that benchmark far outstretched the religious Christian sphere and progressively became a focal date for every aspect of Western human culture, including economics, science, and politics. Truthfully, its impact stretched far beyond the West, and still does today.

Meanwhile, new time horizons now engage the adult imagination. We belong to a cosmic creation of at least 13.7 billion years, grounded in the home planet earth for 3.8 billion years, sprung directly from the organic life chain of some 2 billion years. But most daunting of all for many humans — in fact millions are not even aware of it — is a human evolving story of 7 million years (see O'Murchu 2008).[12] Adults today think *big*. It seems to be a survival requirement for this time. More than that, evolution itself seems to be luring us into these new enlarged horizons.

Global warming and other catastrophic disturbances affecting us today alert us to what is becoming an indisputable fact: *everything in creation is interconnected*. We now experience a growing sense that we all belong to the relational web of cosmic and planetary becoming. That web is one, an undivided wholeness; intuitively, we have known that for most of our evolutionary story as a human species. Our immersion in the creative process of planet and cosmos and our interdependent relationship with all created reality form the bedrock of our human identity.

Born of stardust, nourished by the process of photosynthesis, molded from the slime of the earth, our materiality is the basis of our entire existence, including our spirituality. We are creatures of the earth, and it is precisely in our ability to relate meaningfully with the earth that we discover who we really are.

For much of the Christian era — and far longer in some of the other great religions — the goal of the spiritual life was to facilitate our exit from this sinful vale of tears to the fulfillment of a life hereafter. Phrases like "flee the world," "abandon the world," "turn your back on the world" occur frequently in the spiritual manuals. Although we should not equate these words with the material creation, they often led to a dismissive and pejorative understanding of our home planet, which in turn prohibited any possibility of our being able to appreciate and understand the nonvisible (quantum) dimensions of creation that inform and illuminate the spiritual search in our time.

Postcolonial studies help us to understand the undercurrents of this derogatory regard for the created order. The patriarchal urge for control and order surfaces strongly. There is a long history behind the notion of human waywardness, our tendency to behave sinfully and irresponsibly, yet it belongs largely to recent millennia as highlighted in Part One. It is easier to control people when we can label them as deviant. The control is even more justified when we imply that everything in creation has been corrupted because of human waywardness (the theory of original sin).

And a deadly consequence of this dominating urge is its narrow anthropocentric focus. *Humans alone matter.* Humans are masters of everything else in creation, which means that creation is an object for human use and disposal — but only as directed by those in charge. We begin to encounter a frightening level of disconnection: life on earth is superficial; cosmology is of no consequence (despite the fact that every religion claims that God created the universe). The only thing that matters is the salvation of the human soul — and only humans have souls!

Despite this anti-world vision, every religion witnesses saints and mystics who succeeded in breaking through the negative denunciation and have integrated their spirituality with the natural world around them. In Christianity, St. Francis of Assisi, Meister Eckhart, and a number of women mystics (e.g., Hildegarde of Bingen, Mechtild of Magdeburg, Julian of Norwich) discovered deep spiritual meaning in the workings of the larger creation. The collaborative research of Mary Evelyn Tucker and her husband, John Grim (see online *www.religionandecology.org/About/founders.php*), provide inspiring examples of this mystical integration across the great world religions and also in the traditions of indigenous (first nation) peoples. In the West the cleavage between the sacred and the secular became particularly accentuated in the seventeenth, eighteenth, and nineteenth centuries due to the rise of Jansenism in Europe. By the mid-twentieth century the tide had begun to turn significantly, thanks to new scientific breakthroughs and various spiritual awakenings from "the ground up" as the Spirit began to blow afresh over the mold-ridden edifice of the spirituality of domination and control.

An Enlarged Context

In the latter half of the twentieth century, spirituality progressively became an interdisciplinary field of study, into which more and more people were able to bring their adult selves, having upended the debilitating cycle of codependency. Psychology was one of the first transforming influences. In due course *cosmology* (what some called creation spirituality) was to make an even greater impact. Anthropology illuminated aspects of the human story long ignored or forgotten (see O'Murchu 2008). Multi-faith dialogue gave birth to enculturation. A new synthesis came to the fore. It is still taking shape, and gradually weaving a cultural identity of its own. Adults are beginning to claim a grounding in reality robbed from us for millennia, hence the emergence of the protean person, reviewed in previous chapters.

This novel approach is often described as *The New Story* (Swimme and Berry 1992; Primack and Abrams 2007; Hathaway and Boff 2009; Cannato 2006; 2010). In fact it is a very old story being reclaimed afresh. Some of its features look very new but have already been known to our species going back over millennia in evolution's great story.

1. *Aliveness:* Throughout the patriarchal era of recent millennia, humans alone were deemed to be fully alive (and men more than women), bestowing the consequent right to dominate and control the dead inert matter of creation. Both science and spirituality are now pointing us in a radically different direction. Aliveness belongs primarily to the cosmic creation, and from that source it is bestowed on every organism. Human aliveness is *a derived way* of being alive, and without the aliveness of the greater dimensions (cosmos and earth planet) we humans would cease to exist. We are totally dependent for our life and well-being on the creation that surrounds us.

2. *Relationality.* The creation to which we belong is not so much a material object as an embodied web of intricate relationships, an interdependent process forever evolving in more highly complex and creative ways. It is from this relational matrix that everything is brought into being and sustained throughout its existence. The capacity to relate — which for humans translates into the call to cooperate (see Margulis 1998; Hrdy 2009) — is the dynamism through which everything grows and flourishes. And as we shall see later, it is also endowed with paradox, a sense of bafflement and contradiction that human rational thought cannot fully comprehend.

3. *Spirituality.* Indigenous people have long had the intuition of creation being infused by "The Great Spirit." Something akin to spirit-power underpins the entire cosmic web, energizing and enlivening the organic and chemical processes at the heart of all growth. Although speculation about the Great Spirit is assumed to belong to some primitive religiosity — animism, paganism, or whatever we care to call it — it appears that for our ancient ancestors, the notion carried a far deeper and more integrated meaning. It was linked to religion only in more recent millennia, probably to satisfy the patriarchal urge for more definitive control over the information. Spirituality has long been known to our ancestors and predates religion by thousands of years.

4. *Emergence* (Story). Thus there evolved, over at least a few million years, an understanding that creation is not so much about discrete material entities, but rather should be understood as a story of creativity and complexity, evolving in accordance with an innate, inner intelligence. The process seems to have meaning and direction written into it, a rationale that rational humans cannot grasp clearly at this time, a wisdom we might never be able to master fully. Today the story has become conscious in us humans, giving the cosmic, planetary narrative a new depth of coherence and meaning, but not the right for us humans to reserve the story to our own conquering advantage.

5. *Revelation.* Long before religions ever evolved, long before dogmatic theologians became preoccupied with the uniqueness of

the historical Jesus, long before ardent religionists pitched the religions against one another with violent intent, God was activating and revealing an embracing sense of mystery in the creative unfolding of creation itself. Creation is the primordial scripture revealing something of the divine intent. And when we glimpse this insight it also becomes obvious that the story continues to unfold. Today we humans are key players (but not masters) in that endeavor.

The Bewildering Paradox

The late John Wheeler suggests that we live in a participatory universe: we are part of the universe that is a work in progress. This requires of us, however, the maturity and wisdom to take the good and the bad alike, because both elements exist — and apparently always will — in an evolving universe.

From a human point of view, creation looks fragile, precarious, and problematic. Indeed, as Charles Foster (2009) illustrates so vividly, the violence and wanton destructability so apparent in organic life almost overwhelms our search for meaning in the larger web of life. Introducing his book on suffering, Joseph Amato (1990, 2) reminds us that "The fossil record of millions of years reveals the irreducible place of pain and suffering in life. As the first plants and animals emerged on the earth, parasitic microorganisms were waiting for them." Unfortunately he fails to point out the more complex interdependent processes whereby those same microorganisms contribute to the coevolution of organic matter in significant ways.

From our conventional viewpoint, everything has to fight for its survival, and in the ensuing battle the strong win while the weak lose out. Storms, hurricanes, tornados, typhoons batter and bruise the creation around us. Even in the vast space of the extraterrestrial world, we know of much turmoil and chaos as planetary organisms crash into each other in a continuous cycle of cataclysmic dispersal. With good reason, we wonder what is the meaning of it all!

Adults of our time no longer look to the religions to help unravel these imponderable contradictions. Today suggestions of a fundamental flaw, requiring redemption by divine intervention, make little or no sense to reflective people. Such arguments feel like explaining things away rather than procuring some semblance of a meaningful explanation. Instead, contemporary adults tend to look to the big story of creation to throw light on our inherited predicaments. A new intuitive awakening seems to be taking place, with a strange blend of the mystical and the scientific, leading the seeker in quite a different direction from former times.

For billions of years now — long before the human species ever evolved — the cosmic creation has unfolded and flourished. Not much evolved in a linear, deterministic fashion, nor did much progress happen without a great deal of chaos and destruction. This is what some modern cosmologists call *the paradox of creation-and-destruction* (see Swimme and Berry 1992).

The Cycle of Creation-and-Destruction

The paradox is best explained by a simple diagram (below), showing the cycle of upward and downward curves, the upward representing creation and the downward representing destruction. The cycles continue repeating — unceasingly it seems. Has it been like this since the beginning of time? Yes, it seems so. Is God behind all this? Religionists might answer affirmatively. However, postulating God at this stage may jeopardize rather than reinforce the deep, ancient wisdom being explored.

Instead, we need to see the paradox as an innate dimension of the cosmic evolutionary process itself. More importantly, we need to realize that without this paradox nothing would exist. What to humans looks like a gross contradiction is basic to the creation, sustenance, and flourishing of everything in our universe. Already the reader may begin to glimpse that there is more to suffering than what meets the human eye. And only this broad explanatory foundation makes sense for a growing number of adults in the modern world.

Engaging Paradox

First comes the paradox! The *Concise Oxford Dictionary* defines "paradox" as "a person or thing conflicting with preconceived notions of what is reasonable or possible." A paradox does not make sense to our rational minds. A paradox captivates a surplus of meaning that cannot be contained within the structure of rational discourse. For an adult spirituality of our time this is a crucial issue. Adults today are rarely satisfied with compelling rational explanations; there is a "surplus of meaning" that transcends rationality, yet to mature adults it feels essential in our search for deeper meaning. The ability to embrace paradox is central to this sense of maturity.

This is my favored definition of a paradox: "it is a contradiction, with meaning written underneath it." Our commonsense, rational world is being contradicted. We are forced into a double-bind that does not fit with our inherited expectations. The more we try to rationalize it — make sense of it in terms of rational daily experience — the more weird and baffling it becomes.

The meaning, therefore, is not on the surface. It is hidden from the immediacy of our gaze. In fact, it requires a different quality of wisdom — and perception — to make it accessible. And we cannot resolve (or solve) a paradox. As with the koan of Zen Buddhism, we must learn to befriend it; or better still, we need to allow the paradox to befriend us.

An example from the Christian scriptures may be helpful: "For when I am weak, then I am strong" (2 Cor. 12:10). Weakness and strength are perceived to be opposites; the one contradicts the other. In the world of daily experience, one cannot be strong and weak at the same time. Yet many among us can intuit a level of meaning. Some will recall times of sickness, trauma, even breakdown that led to new life, hope, and meaning. Beneath the overt statement is an unspoken alternative logic that points to a significance and depth that is not immediately obvious in the words as spoken or read.

We now return to the dynamic that seems to underpin everything in creation (including humans) and operates at the level of large galactic spheres but also at the micro level of bacteria and cells. Destruction and fresh creation are often intertwined in the unfolding story of evolution. They seem to need each other. Between 1994 and 2004, scholars traced the course of hurricanes across the Atlantic Ocean, noting that where the hurricanes were most severe are precisely the places today where we have the richest growth on the bed of the ocean. Destruction and creation sitting side-by-side.

A Recurring Cycle

Another way of naming the cyclic process is that of *birth–death–rebirth*. Old realities often have to die — fade into the twilight — to make way for the new, although logically there is no reason why the old and new cannot coexist. In evolutionary terms, new breakthroughs are often quite different from their predecessors, although in terms of cumulative breakthrough what was achieved through the former organisms is contained also in the new expressions. The new, however, thrives primarily through that which is authentically novel, and not by clinging on to the exemplary models of the past.

The concept of death is particularly problematic for our contemporaries, and many still regard it with a type of codependent passivity. Whether from a religious or secular perspective, death is seen as an aberration that one day we hope to get rid of. In evolutionary terms, *death is a life stage,* absolutely essential to growth and development. Once again, we are defying rationality. And not merely rationality, but the long tradition of popular spirituality. According to St. Paul, death came into the world through human moral transgression (Rom. 5:12ff); for St. Paul, death is the consequence of sin, a perception still widely adopted by evangelical religionists.

Before we can hope to address the problem of suffering, we need to stop demonizing death. Death is an integral and essential dimension in the evolution of life — at every level. Without death, everything would be dead. Death is not, and never has been, a consequence of sin. Death did not begin with human moral transgression. Death has always existed and always will. Death is a necessary good, not an evil. There certainly prevail many forms of meaningless death in the modern world, but that is a human-invented problem, often ensuing from a lack of adult maturity, insight, and wisdom.

Throughout the landscape of creation we witness the unceasing process of new life evolving, growing, and developing, reaching its maturation, and then entering into a declining phase culminating in extinction or death. In some cases there is a direct link between the death of the old and the new life, as in the case of seeds fermenting and blossoming forth as new plants. In other cases, death seems to be a precursor for new life, but not necessarily connected in any direct way. Once again, we need to remember, we are dealing with a paradoxical process that does not make full rational sense. There is more to life than rational logic.

Suffering as Paradox

If, therefore, there is a quality of suffering that is innate to creation as a central feature of the evolutionary process, how do we distinguish between meaningful and meaningless suffering? This is a perennial question for contemporary adults. If an earthquake is essential to the earth's growth and development, is the consequent death of two hundred thousand people a wanton and capricious outcome of a paradoxical evolutionary system in which humans — and presumably other creatures — are totally at the mercy of cosmic forces or at the mercy of a capricious God? If hurricanes can stir up rich mineral materials in the bed of the Atlantic Ocean producing wonderfully rich and elegant plant life, how do we reconcile that with the destruction reaped in New Orleans through the hurricane of August 2005 or the devastating earthquake in Haiti in January 2010?

It is both congruent and necessary for adults in our time to pose such questions. And adults are not interested in naïve answers, particularly of the pseudo-religious type, whether adopting the notion of a mysterious act of God, or worse still some kind of divine punitive intervention. Paradoxes tend not to yield to rational logical answers, nor is it responsible to be postulating a punitive, capricious God to explain the dilemma (see Sobrino 2004, 137ff). According to John F. Haught (2006, 188), "Suffering is the dark side of any universe that remains unfinished and in which anticipation remains alive." We need to seek out a deeper wisdom through which we can pose more discerning questions. How we interrogate the material at hand will determine how enlightening and helpful the response will be.

The tsunami of December 2004 is a particularly useful example, offering significant insights on how adults could engage the power of paradox. On December 25, 2004, the Pacific Tsunami Warning Center (PTWC) in Hawaii signaled a major earthquake brewing in the Indian Ocean. This piece of technology is among the most sophisticated humans have developed to read earthquake activity. Scientists working at the base acted promptly, transferring the appropriate signals to the countries they discerned to be under greatest threat: Thailand, Indonesia and Australia.

None of the countries had responded within the statutory timespan. The scientists then resorted to ordinary telephones in order to contact the designated government departments, using information provided by the countries in question. But nobody seemed to be at home to answer the telephones. Presumably all had gone on holiday for Christmas. Meanwhile, the tsunami struck, creating havoc and massive destruction to humans and landscape alike. Our human technology failed us badly.

It is worth comparing this episode with the 1975 earthquake in the city of Taiching in Taiwan. The available technology was considerably inferior to that which we have today in Hawaii. It was signaling a major earthquake for the city of Taiching; worse still it was predicting that the epicenter was likely to be in the heart of the city itself, home to some ninety thousand people.

Local government authorities were in quite a quandary. The technology at hand had not been very accurate on previous occasions. Evacuating ninety thousand people was a major undertaking and might subsequently prove to have been unnecessary. Would they take a risk and do nothing? But then if the earthquake did hit the city, and they had not acted appropriately, how would they ever reconcile their consciences?

They reviewed all their options, knowing that it was a race against time. Somebody suggested that scouts be sent out to observe the animals, and make note of how they were behaving. Some ridiculed the very idea. However, it was finally agreed to do so and volunteers quickly came forth. In less than an hour the animal-observers were back, having noted that all the animals in the city had moved, or were moving, to higher ground. This was compelling evidence!

A decision was made to evacuate the city. Quite a panic, and at times rather chaotic, but everybody was relocated just in time as the earthquake rocked the city, causing extensive damage and wrecking much of the city-center infrastructure. Not a single person lost their life.

The comparison between 2004 and 1975 is intriguing and of crucial importance to understand the paradox we are exploring. In 2004, we relied solely on human technology, and it failed us dismally. In 1975 we combined the existing technology with the innate wisdom of nature, and it paid dividends. Whereas rational knowledge on its own was unable to protect us against the destructive power of the paradox, intuitive wisdom empowered us to befriend the paradox, thus enabling us to protect human life.

As indicated above, a paradox cannot be rationally explained but we can engage it to our own advantage, and perhaps also to the advantage of other aspects of life. The tsunami has left us with a rich reservoir of stories that reinforce the role of intuitive wisdom in learning to befriend life's great paradoxes. I share one of the many parabolic-type stories, this one related to the Morgan fisherfolk off the southwest coast of Thailand, who on the morning of December 26, 2004, noticed that the familiar sea waters had receded far beyond their usual limits. Things felt off kilter. Nature was not at ease.

These primitive people — with no formal schooling or education — spend their entire time fishing and live in simple hovels along the coastline. Fish is their daily diet, fishing their lifelong occupation. They looked intently upon those receding waters and upon the fishes leaping anxiously. They consulted their elders and in union with them quickly reached a collective decision: they intuitively knew within hours that massive waves would break upon their shoreline.

They gathered their meager possessions and headed for the hills. On the way they met a group of Western tourists, some of whom ridiculed their story. But a few took them seriously and accompanied them to further heights. Thanks to those Westerners we have inherited this amazing story. Those who dismissed and ridiculed their silly tale walked right into the eye of the storm and lost their lives. The fisherfolk and their accompanying visitors were totally safe!

Most of the meaningless suffering we encounter is actually caused by wrong human intervention, more accurately by *human ignorance*. And most of it could be resolved if humans learned to befriend creation's paradox in a more informed and enlightened way. There is no point in waiting for some divine rescuer to do it for us. The empowering "Great Spirit" has endowed us with all the resources we need to live meaningfully on planet earth. We don't know how to appropriate or use those resources because we are so alienated from the living creation itself. The Morgan fisher-folk knew how to respond in such a way that kept meaningless suffering to a minimum. We all could do the same if we were as earth-connected as they are.

Religious explanations for pain and suffering in the world no longer carry credibility for growing numbers of protean adults. These explanations feel like rationalizations that explain away rather than explain our dilemma. In a paradoxical universe there will always be untidy, chaotic dimensions that cannot be explained in a humanly satisfactory way, but when people become more coherently grounded within the paradox, then the kind of explanation they seek, and the kind that makes more intellectual and spiritual sense, is very different from many of the conventional religious explanations.

Adult people of faith have lost faith in the God of the gaps. They reason, "Why should a higher wisdom come to our rescue? It is we ourselves who created the problem; it is up to us to resolve it!" We have been blessed and endowed with the resources and resilience to bring about a different quality of engagement with the creation to which we integrally belong. Adults today strive to trust their innate endowments. And progressively they are becoming more aware of their earth-based and cosmic responsibilities. The big obstacle they confront is institutional resistance. It is the cultural cancer of our time.

Much of our human codependency is related to the institutions that daily impinge upon our lives. Mainline governments, market forces, political alliances, global corporations, religious institutions, educational establishments, and many more, are distinctly out of sync with the new adult consciousness of our time. They operate systems of control, with at best a subdued sense of trust. They breed codependency on an enormous scale, evoking passivity, anger, and a range of violent counterreactions. They pacify the masses but fail to deliver anything resembling real happiness or fulfillment for adult people. Another way — a third way? — must be envisioned.

Revisiting the Paradox

Our desire for a pain-free world, devoid of depletion and destruction, actually arises from a false sense of adulthood. It portrays the adult as ruler and overlord rather than one who engages convivially and cooperatively with evolution's unfoldings. More authentic adulthood acknowledges our inherent belonging to the web of life, an integration in which we — and everything else in creation — grow and develop through the open-ended and consequent untidiness of our evolutionary universe, and not in spite of them. Mature adulthood can live with this incompleteness and work with it. Indeed, without this messy landscape there would be no true freedom and no space for real creativity. In all probability it is the best of all possible worlds, precisely because it is in process, unfinished and imperfect.

From an adult perspective, therefore, suffering is not simply an evil to be got rid of. A certain quality and degree of suffering is essential to an evolving universe. The adult task therefore is not to try to rid the world of suffering, a strategy that almost certainly will exacerbate the suffering that already exists, but to discern which forms of suffering are necessary for evolutionary growth and development as distinct from those which are caused by inappropriate human inter-ference, the type that typically militate against creation's wholesome unfolding.

Indigenous peoples have long recognized a fundamental mystery at the heart of creation. In a range of mythic stories and ritual cere-monies they strive not to eliminate the paradoxes of creation, but to befriend them in a way that honors their paradoxical nature, while also seeking a deeper wisdom on how these paradoxes can serve the well-being of humankind. This is more akin to the adult engagement with reality I am exploring in the present chapter.

The language of paradox is written all over creation. It is there for us to read and discern. When we do attend to it, it seems to make life more tolerable, bearable, dare I suggest more meaningful. When we fail to attend, we expose ourselves to forces that can be cruel and devastating. Apparently, we do have a choice. The big problem, how-ever, is that the choice seems to lead in directions that are alien to our imperial Western consciousness; to our rational ways of perceiving and acting; to our prized sense of being in control of the contingent nature of the world we inhabit. To opt for the other choice — follow the "stupid" fisherfolk — defies our intelligence and common sense. It feels like betraying or abandoning all we have worked so hard for, all that constitutes the very foundations of a civilized world.

The perennial question, therefore, relates to the suffering we humans cause and exacerbate, because apparently we have lacked the wisdom to read the great paradoxes of life in a more enlight-ened way. Just imagine a human civilization in which the wisdom of the Morgan fisherfolk was extensively practiced. I suspect there would still be a lot of pain, suffering, and contradiction around, but we would deal with them in a more discerning way and manage the outcomes with greater care and sensitivity.

It boils down to two foundational human outlooks: *control* or *trust.* Our human urge to dominate and control may well be the great-est single liability of our so-called civilized world. Often the more we try to control, the more everything seems to be out of control, which in turn drives us to be more controlling. Our desire for control becomes compulsive, one other among the numerous addictions that plague humanity today, one highlighted some years ago in a semi-nal work of the systems therapist Anne Wilson-Schaef; she concludes with these words (Wilson-Schaef 1987, 145):

> The Addictive System encourages addictions to keep people so far away from their feelings and awareness that they cannot challenge the system. Unfortunately (or fortunately), more and more people whose lives are being destroyed by addictions are starting to seek help. They are aligning themselves with recovery groups and starting to recover. The further along they get in their recovery, the less able they are to support and participate in the Addictive System. In other words, in many ways the system contains within itself the seeds of its own destruction. This is the great cosmic joke and, to me, a hopeful sign.

Adults of our time know that control is not the solution; trust is. To make that shift, however, is a momentous undertaking. Our competitive, brutalized world is not amenable to the spirit of trust. Our cultural compulsiveness requires everybody to be a winner — and all of the time. There is little tolerance for losers, for vulnera-bility, for weakness. Losers feel everybody is out to undermine their hopes; they trust nobody. But the winners do not trust either, except the select few that play their collusive games of domination, power, and control. Within this quagmire — engineered by humans — is an intensity of pain and suffering that defies all rationality.

In the past, and among major institutions of the present time, we hoped that some higher wisdom would resolve it for us. But that naivety is rapidly evaporating. Fortunately, we don't have to start from scratch. The emerging consciousness of recent decades has already been birthing the new adult consciousness, cocreating new structural possibilities to embody a more dynamic way of relating to our world. We will review these in subsequent chapters.

(a) **Conventional inherited wisdom** *minimizes the God-given context of our creativity, virtually ignoring the cosmos, viewing our existence on earth as spiritually problematic, offering one*

basic solution to our human dilemma: salvation in a world
beyond.

(b) **Embedded codependency** begets a pervasive sense of unworthiness, hindering humans from their adult, cocreative
responsibilities as cosmic-planetary creatures.

(c) **Adult empowerment** requires us to cherish, protect, and
promote every dimension of our being as cosmic, earthy
creatures called to engage proactively in building up the whole
of God's creation, including the precarious dimensions of an
essentially paradoxical universe.

Chapter Twelve

Embracing Embodied Relationality

FOCUS: Universal life is not governed by the competitive dynamics of Darwinian evolution but by the interdependent connections formed by the relational matrix from which everything emanates. Reconnecting with this relational web is essential for health and well-being.

> *Our modern hunger to belong is particularly intense. An increasing majority of people feel no belonging. We have fallen out of rhythm with life. The art of belonging is the recovery of the wisdom of rhythm.*
> — JOHN O'DONOHUE

QUANTUM PHYSICS HIGHLIGHTS the inherent relationality (interconnectedness) of all living things. We humans inherit this tendency in our capacity for relationships. Conventionally, we think first of our relationships with other people, but in truth relationship defines all our interaction with life — at every level from the cosmic sphere to that of the symbiotic interplay of the bacterial world (see Lynn Margulis 1998). In a word, we are programed to relate, a fact that is difficult to comprehend or accept in a world so ridden with strife, competition, estrangement, and violence.

Our relationality is mediated primarily through our bodies. As embodied creatures we connect with every other embodied form in the planetary web of life. The body is the site in which many worlds meet and seek out a meaningful synthesis. Although we are programed to interconnect, it is an onerous and perilous task, mainly because of centuries of negative moralistic conditioning.

For all religions, the body is suspect to one degree or another. It is the soul that is real, not the body. And the body is frequently portrayed as a hindrance to the soul, and its destiny to be redeemed and saved. This dualistic split no longer makes sense to growing numbers of contemporary adults. Today, we view the body as a unified process, seeking to evolve into fuller realization within the larger embodied spheres of earth and cosmos. Salvation is a process of integration rather than one of escape to a life hereafter.

Central to our life experience as embodied creatures is our sexual creativity. This erotic core defines the very essence of our humanity, yet no other sphere of human life has been so demonized and subjected to moralistic denunciation. In this sphere more than any other, human adults face formidable challenges for integration and more authentic growth (see Farley 2008; Whitehead and Whitehead 2009).

First, the Body

Dealing meaningfully with the body has been a struggle for humans for quite a long time, but probably for not as long as is widely assumed. Our prehistoric ancestors, living in a more convivial way with the surrounding environment, probably experienced an embodied connectedness with life that has been subverted or lost in more recent millennia. Our culture of patriarchal dominance, the ways we prioritize rational discourse, and a widespread tendency to commodify the surrounding creation all contribute to a progressive alienation of the body and our relationship to it. The more we try to conquer and control the earth body, on the misguided assumption that it would give us more power, the more we problematize the human body, to levels of alienation that pervert the very meaning of our existence as cosmic-planetary creatures.

Religion, too, has played quite a destructive role in the sense that all the major religions we know today evolved during a timespan heavily committed to patriarchal advancement. Religion was extensively used to control life, specifically human initiative. This resulted in the problematizing of the body, progressively leading to the demonization of the body. We see this reflected in the following passage from St. Paul's Letter to the Romans (7:18–25):

I know of nothing good living in me — living, that is, in my unspiritual self — for though the will to do what is good is in me, the performance is not, with the result that instead of doing the good things I want to do, I carry out the sinful things I do not want. When I act against my will then, it is not my true self doing it, but sin which lives in me.

In fact, this seems to be the rule, that every single time I want to do good it is something evil that comes to hand. In my inmost self I dearly love God's law, but I can see that my body follows a different law which my reason dictates. This is what makes me a prisoner of that law of sin which lives inside my body.

What a wretched man I am! Who will rescue me from this body doomed to death?

Volumes have been written on the writings of St. Paul, predominantly by male scholars with varying degrees of investment in, and commitment to, the Christian faith. Consequently, most commentators try to cast the writings of Paul in a positive light, highlighting nuances that will escape most readers and preachers and clearly will not impress fundamentalists who like to quote literally and liberally from the writings of sacred scripture. As with any classical text, there are subtle and profound meanings that will escape the average reader (Christian). For the purposes of this book, I am using the above passage as understood and appropriated in popular, conventional Christian culture. My reflections may not do justice to deeper Pauline insight, since I am examining the text for its popular impact, not for its deeper meaning.

At its face value the above passage presents quite a distorted view of human embodiment, a view that has seriously hampered and even undermined adult growth in faith. These are some of the distortions I allude to:

1. The dualistic split between the inner and the outer, between the spiritual and the unspiritual, undermines a more fundamental unity that characterizes human embodiment.

2. Rationality is then invoked to separate the two realms, to diminish the one and exalt the other. The process is typically depicted with the violent metaphor of "a battle."

3. Death is demonized as a consequence of what is assumed to be a normative anthropology when in truth it is a distorted false understanding. Death is not an evil, but an integral dimension of the universal dynamic of birth–death–rebirth.

4. This conflictual image has a particular appeal to the rational male psyche and has been extensively internalized by women due to male patriarchal conditioning. The metaphor of the robust hero is deeply embedded in this anthropology.

5. An inflated anthropocentrism underlies the entire description: human beings are deemed to be superior to everything else in creation and, therefore, should be capable of sorting out the deficiencies that prevent them from being totally in charge and fully in control.

6. A more wholesome anthropology would acknowledge that humans share in creation's great paradox (pp. 128–137) as does every other organism. To engage the paradox with creativity and freedom ensues in a quality of untidiness that every organism (including humans) must learn to live with. Mastery resolves nothing and it fails to acknowledge the untidiness required for creativity and freedom.

7. A more humble and humane anthropology accepts human limitation, not as a deficiency, but a necessary dimension *of paradox*. A greater transparency toward tolerance, forbearance, forgiveness, and healing is what will empower humans to live with dignity and integrity and not the harsh moralistic judgments that often ensue as applications of the passage from the letter to the Romans quoted above.

8. The human is portrayed as superior, dominant, and isolated. He (the ideal human is male) stands alone over and against all reality. This may well be the fundamental distortion, totally ignoring (it seems) fact that humans are programed to relate,

and it is in exercising our capacity for relationships that we live at our best (not perfectly) — in our relationships with one another, with other organic creatures, with the earth planet, and with the cosmos.

The demonization of the body has haunted Christianity for quite a long time. Women feel the pain in a particularly severe way. Not surprising when we learn that "Western cultural discourse regards the human body as classical or grotesque. In medieval culture, the classical body was male, harmonious, unified, proportionate, spiritual, and pure; it was free of pain, limitation, or decay. Women and other marginalized social groups and classes were associated with the grotesque body with its material orifices, fluids, and filth. As representatives of the grotesque body women were disproportionate, heterogeneous, profane, sinful, congenitally impure, and deserving of punishment" (Lanzetta 2005, 157–58).

Adults of our time seek to reclaim the body and restore its wisdom and spirituality into a more holistic synthesis. And this is not merely a personal and interpersonal challenge. It embraces far wider implications, which are systemic, ecological, planetary, and cosmic all at once. The web of life, which empowers and challenges us to relate, far outstretches our human, interpersonal domain. Indeed, the propensity to relate belongs primarily to creation (chapter 10) and not just to the human species.

Programed to Relate

For millions of years, our ancestors remained very close to nature, a quality of *conviviality* that sustained their every endeavor for meaningful embodiment. Theirs was a quality of mutuality that defies many cultural norms of our time. They were not slaves to nature as we often assume, but collaborated with the organicity of universal life in ways that benefited the development of the human and nonhuman alike. Our ancestors did not even think of conquering or controlling nature, because they viewed the natural world as a benign organism from which every resource emanated. And perhaps most disturbing of all for contemporary rationalists, our ancient ancestors perceived the entire web of life to be infused with the power of the Great Spirit.

In that cosmic-planetary enterprise, interrelationship was the primary mode of engagement. We could say that everything was programed to relate — a claim that should not be construed as deterministic. Even in the midst of powerful destruction, through storms and other calamities, the sense of relationality endured. Today the scientific culture seeks to subdue all "irregularity" to human subjection and control. Our ancient ancestors adopted a different outlook and approach. To them, the great paradox of birth–death–rebirth permeated every dimension of creation, a paradox they sought to befriend rather than a fundamental flaw to be rid of. Without the paradox, creativity would also cease to be. Long before formal education or religion, our ancestors understood the paradox and learned to live with its bewildering wisdom.

In the religious sphere we use the notion of discernment to figure out how best to respond to God (or to life) in times of major crisis or challenge. The religions deem this to be a skill unique to adult people of great holiness and deeply versed in the sacred tradition of one or other of the great religions. It seems to me that the Morgan fisherfolk on the morning of December 26, 2004, did a brilliant piece of discernment. Yet they had no training or expertise in religious learning, nor would our Western civilization consider them adult in the normative use of the word. I suspect many learned, religious people would dismiss them as ignorant pagans. I recall a great statement of the scripture scholar John Dominic Crossan, which aptly reinforces these insights: "My point is not that those ancient people told literal stories and we are now smart enough to take them symbolically, but that they told them symbolically and we are now dumb enough to take them literally" (Crossan and Watts 1996, 60ff).

The Morgan fisherfolk live out of a deep sense of grounding in their environment. They relate intimately, not just interpersonally, but with the entire web of life that sustains, guides, and nourishes their every endeavor. Paradoxically, their ability to relate with the surrounding environment is probably more skilful than their ability to relate with other humans, their own tribespeople included. The relational web of life thrives on a degree and quality of mutuality that cannot be reduced to the dynamics of human relationships. Creation handles relationality far more effectively than humans do; some indigenous peoples engage paradox with a wisdom and ingenuity far in excess of our normative cultural expectations.

Embodied Sexuality

Because we are relational creatures, the urge and desire toward sexual intimacy is innate to who we are as embodied persons. We cannot escape being sexual. Our sexuality defines the very essence of our humanity. It is the erotic wellspring that connects us deeply not merely with other humans but with every creature with which we share the planetary web of life. Here we touch into adult yearnings that are particularly acute, and even explosive, at this time.

Two terms need particular attention: "sexuality" and "the erotic." They are intimately connected. Sexuality is popularly understood as sexual intercourse, and most human cultures regard it as the unique prerogative of a heterosexual couple. Our inherited understanding (mainly from Aristotle) is heavily infiltrated with biology: sex is a biological mechanism for the procreation of new life. Conventional Catholicism and modern Islam tend to adopt a literal interpretation of this rationale.

The erotic tends to be described as the ability to arouse sexual feeling and awaken sexual curiosity, sensationalized through advertising and a range of commodities that evoke ever greater need fulfillment. In religious terms, the erotic is often depicted as sexual temptation, and the avenue through which original sin is transmitted down through the ages. The erotic is a dangerous instinctual drive, to be guarded with great vigilance and forever subject to the bar of reason and rationality.

These are dangerously misguided understandings, which quite rightly are rejected by many people in the contemporary world. However, we do concede that those who reject the inherited wisdom are often unsure what they are seeking instead. A great deal of confusion prevails, sometimes leading to dysfunctional liaisons which can leave behind a trail of pain, anguish, broken hearts, and broken lives.

Sexuality does not belong primarily to our genitals, and therefore it is not primarily about genital behavior. Neither is our sex-drive/desire activated solely in our brains. Our sexual energy inhabits our entire embodied selves and stretches beyond the boundaries of the individual toward connection beyond the individualized self. Our sexual, erotic energy can also be evoked by factors outside and beyond the individual person.

Human sexuality may be defined as *the sum total of our feelings, moods, and emotions as mediated through social interaction.* Physical contact is the first medium through which the child channels sexual energy. In the adult sphere, friendship is the first resource, a developmental process very much underestimated in our oversexualized world. We tend to bypass the friendship stage(s) in our cultural compulsiveness to become sexually involved. Already in teenage years, many people today engage in genital sexual behavior.

Today, human sexuality is a complex issue and a bewildering one for many adults — with few "safe" places to explore the more urgent issues. New sexual freedoms are embraced on a universal scale, with the blame attributed to reckless secularism and the ensuing promiscuity in our time. In my opinion, this is an erroneous explanation, but a convenient one to avoid a more bitter truth: the reckless freedom is a direct, albeit subconscious retort, to the widespread sexual repression of earlier times. The overemphasis on sex-as-biology, with the primary goal of procreation, is the root cause of the hedonistic culture of sex for *recreation.* The two phenomena are intimately connected.

However, the sexual revolution is not merely a reaction to a dysfunctional past. It is also an evolutionary catalyst pointing us to a future that will be different — and chaotic for a long time to come. Religiously and politically, socially and economically, monogamous heterosexual marriage is still widely recognized as the "official" outlet for the expression and articulation of sexual intimacy. Yet few can deny that is a rapidly changing landscape raising several bewildering questions for church and state alike.

Human sexuality no longer belongs to the enclave of the hetero-sexual monogamous married couple. Homosexual expressions are widely adopted today. Millions of couples cohabit rather than marry. Lifelong relationships are difficult to sustain. And most bewildering of all, human sexuality is extensively used for pornographic and glitzy advertising, strongly impacting on minds and psyches of many vulnerable people.

How to make sense of this complex landscape is the challenge facing growing numbers of contemporary adults. Some suspect that a new understanding of human sexuality is coming to birth, an articulation where biology and procreation will not hold pride of place. In fact, they did not hold primary significance for most of our evolutionary history as a human species. Sexuality was understood primarily as a vehicle for creativity (with procreation as one expression) and for spirituality (as seen in various ancient artistic depictions).

Like all major evolutionary shifts, we can expect that this transition will also be characterized by breakdown and the inevitable confusion and pain that follow. However, because we are dealing with a subject so close to the human heart, so intimate and personal, and for so long consigned to the realm of toxic secrecy, it is not easy to embrace the more public discourse that is now needed to face questions of enormous import for the future of humanity, and specifically for adult people at this time.

What Would Adult Eroticism Look Like?

In a seminal and inspiring work, James and Evelyn Whitehead (2009) propose that a rehabilitation of *eros* is one of the most urgent undertakings confronting humanity today. It will help to repair the emotional and psychic damage of the past while also mobilizing our resources to honor the complexity and challenge of what is unfolding for the future.

The guardians of traditional values, religious and otherwise, suggest that what we need is less eros, not more. "Erotic" has become a loaded word, largely with negative intent, and of all the words pertaining to psychosexual growth, it is the one that needs most careful and creative discernment to resurface a more authentic meaning.

The *erotic* is what sustains and guides our psychosexual energy, with the deep desire for bonding and intimate connection. This is the underlying energy of human sexuality, which the ancient Greek philosophers described as a cosmic power of harmony and life, and which Plato described as the yearning of the human soul for union with the Divine.

The Jewish scholar Philo of Alexandria (30 B.C.E.–40 C.E.) translated the central command of Judaism — to love God with all one's mind, heart, and strength — not with the word *agape,* but with *eros.* Throughout the Middle Ages, Christian mystics like St. Bernard and St. Teresa, along with Muslim Sufi mystics like Ibn al-Farid, Rumi, and Ibn'Arb i, often adopted erotic language and images to describe their passion for God.

Two writers of the twentieth century frequently cited on this topic are C. S. Lewis (1960) and Anders Nygren (1983). Lewis is known for his description of the four loves, namely, affection, friendship, eros, and charity. For Lewis, eros is about "being in love," which in its more mature expression always seeks the good of the other rather than self-absorption, the widely assumed negative connotation. For Nygren, eros is a form of raw appetite, and totally alien to agape, love of the divine. For Freud, Jung, and the theologian Paul Tillich, eros is primarily a unitive force.

In more recent times, Audre Lorde (1984), in an oft-cited essay, claims that the power of the erotic was subverted by the culture of patriarchal control, undermining particularly the creative energy of woman power. Now it needs to be reclaimed, not merely as a gesture of inclusive justice but as the life force that connects and unites across all the barriers and divisions imposed by patriarchal culture.

Adopting Lorde's insights, Carter Heyward (1989, 99) describes the erotic as "our most fully embodied experience of the love of God. As such, it is the source of our capacity for transcendence, the 'crossing over' among ourselves, making connections between ourselves in relation. The erotic is the divine Spirit's yearning, through our body-selves, toward mutually empowering relation, which is our most fully embodied experience of God as love. Regardless of who may be the lovers, the root of the love is sacred movement between and among us."

For Heyward, sexuality may be described as our embodied relational response to sacred/erotic power, a view explored in greater length by Paul Avis (1990) and by the moral theologian Peter Black (2003), who provocatively suggests that a more positive recognition of *eros* is what we need to oust the eroticization of power. Black adopts eight features of the erotic (initially named by the Jewish writer Mordechai Gafni):

1. *Intensity,* an antidote to superficiality and passive aggression.

2. *Pleasurableness*, common to both the erotic and the experience of the holy.

3. Being present to the *infinity of the moment.*

4. *The other as subject,* not object.

5. Radical giving and receiving.

6. *The defining of self,* discovering the self through intimacy with the other.

7. *Overcoming alienation*, as each other opens up to the Other.

8. *Engagement of the creative imagination.* (Black 2003, 122)

One of the biggest challenges facing adults in the twenty-first century is that of relational, psychosexual growth. It is a highly complex subject requiring sensitive and discerning attention. Adults have to deal with the evolving eroticism of today's world not merely for themselves as individuals and in their significant relationships, but also with children, adolescents, and the many situations in which people are entrusted with care for each other. Adult people ponder these issues at great length. They think about them, but frequently experience a deep sense of frustration at the lack of facilities for appropriate dialogue. Apart from the privacy of counseling rooms or the doctor's office, there is a dearth of "safe" places where these pressing and urgent issues can be explored and made the subject of serious adult dialogue. Our culture remains all the poorer for the absence of this discerning adult wisdom.

Programed for Nonviolence?

Relationality, eroticism, sexuality all hint at the value that for most people underpins all others, namely, the power of love. It is the virtue of all virtues and yet one of the most elusive and precarious. And how does one even begin to ponder its deeper meaning in a world that has become so vile and violent? How can we begin to make sense of violence in a world programed for relationality and cooperation? Our embodied reality as human beings remains threatened and vulnerable under the spell of so much pain and irrational suffering.

Volumes have been written on this subject, with most theorists postulating human violence to be a trait inherited from our animal origins.[13] However, ethologists (scholars who study animal behavior) vary considerably on their assessment of animal violence, and some highlight the human tendency to seek out evidence for prevailing theories (a kind of self-fulfilling prophesy). Thus Frans de Waal (2005, 30) highlights how researchers frequently cite examples of violent behavior pertaining to chimpanzees, but rarely allude to the *bonobos* and their distinctive peace-loving interaction:

> Believe me if studies had found that they massacre one another, everybody would know about bonobos. Their peacefulness is the real problem....Bonobos act as if they had never heard of the idea [of violence]. Among bonobos, there's no deadly warfare, little hunting, no male dominance, and enormous amounts of sex.

Margaret Power (1991, 250) reinforces those sentiments when she writes:

> I am aware, that oriented as we in the West are to power, direct competition, initiative and aggressive pursuit of "success" many readers will have — as I had initially — difficulty with the argument that the fundamental adapted form of social

organization of humans and chimpanzees is egalitarian, based on positive behavior, and a relationship of mutual dependence between autonomous actors shifting between fundamental leader-follower status/roles.

Our study of animal and primate behavior is based on some questionable assumptions, including our research strategies. We lock animals in cages for long periods of time and observe a great deal of erratic, aggressive behavior; this is the source of many of our widely held assumptions. Studies of animals in the wild, in their natural environments yield substantially different evidence (Goodall 1986; Power 1991; Fry and Bjorkqvist 1997; Hand 2003).

We also know that animals tend to react aggressively when their habitat is disturbed (see Power 1991, 2). Learning to work collaboratively with the natural animal and primate kingdoms is a painstaking skill, and when embraced, yields evidence pointing much more coherently toward kinship, protection, care, cooperation, and peacemaking. The evidence for aggression and violence is far less impressive. Here we encounter further evidence indicating that our treatment of the human body is always commensurate with how we treat the larger embodied reality of other life forms, including the home planet and the cosmos.

Similarly among humans! According to researcher R. B. Lee (1979), the San people of Africa exhibited virtually no violent behavior prior to 1960. Then the first commissioner of Bushman Affairs was appointed. The natural lifestyle of the tribe was disrupted, often without adequate rationale or explanation. Tensions began to rise, even within the tribe itself, and violence began to escalate. Today the San are considered to be among the most violent tribespeople in Africa.

Stories proliferate of peace-loving people and cultures disrupted and aggravated in the name of development, progress, or modernization. The patriarchal will to dominate can be dangerously misguided. It often lacks the larger context and ability to perceive laterally and in greater depth. Colonization is a subtle process, embedded in an inherited violence that tends to remain subconscious, but in time can become painfully transparent in its cultural and personal impact.

How do we move toward more nonviolent ways of coexistence? A more adult engagement with the great paradoxes of life would empower humans to deal creatively and constructively with our inherited tendency toward violence and destruction. For one thing, embracing the paradox rather than seeking to conquer it would make us a far less violent species. Such engagement would also provide the experiential base for seeing and understanding in a more benign and peace-promoting way. We would then be in a better position to interrogate long-held assumptions that no longer serve us well.

"Man-the-hunter" has been a favorite image of anthropology and palaeontology for quite a long time. It is a favored theory for which there exists little substantial evidence (see Hart and Sussman 2005). It embodies a whole range of contemporary patriarchal projections rather than insights into our ancient past. It reflects the confused status of codependent people of our present time, rather than the wiser "adults" of earlier cultural epochs. Somewhat like the scholarly conviction that we have always been a violent species, our meat-eating is assumed to be the basis of surviving and thriving from earliest times. To the contrary, the evidence for horticulture is far more extensive and substantial than for procuring meat through hunting. In time, we are likely to accrue evidence for widespread vegetarianism and not for extensive meat-eating.

Our destructive ignorance extends far beyond meat-eating. In terms of all foodstuffs, we overproduce, overconsume, and ironically beget a world where millions of our own species are deprived of basic nourishing food. Also alarming is the damage we do to the living earth itself using agricultural practices that undermine the viability of the home planet we inhabit. In the name of our consumptive drivenness, we create an enormous amount of suffering for human and planet alike. More reflective adults know that this is an unsustainable way of living; it simply lacks coherence and meaning.

While other creatures consume in order to connect (and paradoxically there is a sense of violence and destruction involved), we humans consume for the sake of consuming. And the more we consume the more addictive our consumption has become. Something as basic as our eating behavior is grossly dysfunctional, resulting in pain and meaningless suffering for millions, with starvation at one end of the continuum, and obesity (and a range of food-related illnesses) at the other.

The violence that leads to warfare and the other human conflicts that have cost the lives of millions of innocent people throughout the twentieth century, arises from a range of more primitive forms of disconnection. Our cultural dislocation — in terms of the universe, our home planet, the other creatures with whom we share the web of life, even our own species in how we deal with our true story of 7 million years — is at the root of our alienation, our misplaced angst, and our consequent tendency toward violence, animosity, and hatred.

Nonviolence (*ahimsa*) denotes not merely the absence of violence, but a set of dispositions (attitudes or values) that value the inherent goodness of everything in creation and strives to promote the well-being of all sentient beings. This is the formidable task of *justice-making*, without which true embodied love cannot flourish. Indeed, many of the paradoxes that baffle and frighten humans are made all the worse by our inability to befriend paradox; our urge to dominate and control it (often violently) is often what begets the despair and anomie we feel because (as already indicated) it cannot be subjected to human control. Instead of the compulsion for control, we need to redirect our creative energies to learn afresh the skills of right relating, in the name of justice and empowering love. It sounds like we need to start all over again!

For adults of our time this is a daunting challenge, with few inspiring models to reassure or guide us. However, a glimmer of hope is breaking through on the horizon of our pursuit. New filiations, fresh endeavors in human organization, awaken hope. To the fore is the phenomenon of networking, the topic to be explored in our next chapter.

(a) *Conventional inherited wisdom problematizes the body as the site of sin, weakness, and perversity. Humans are encouraged to seek escape from the body-prone-to-corruption. The soul alone can be redeemed and saved.*

(b) **Embedded codependency** *is often manifest in a sense of unworthiness, shame, and ambivalence, sometimes developing into subconscious modes of violent compensations, typically expressed in addictions or compulsions.*

(c) **Adult empowerment** *struggles with how to come home to the body as the primary site of incarnational engagement — through relationality, love, justice, nonviolence. This is one of the most daunting yet empowering challenges confronting adult people of faith today.*

Chapter Thirteen

Adult Governance
in the Power of Networking

FOCUS: Networking looks like the structural model best suited for future empowering, not merely of people but of every life form with which we share planet earth. Networking has enormous potential for evoking adult mutual participation.

Someday, when the grown-ups are back in charge, they'll have quite a mess to clean up.
— PAUL KRUGMAN, *NEW YORK TIMES* COLUMNIST
AND NOBEL LAUREATE

THE POLITICAL LANDSCAPE today presents us with a rather torturous piece of discernment. We have so many models, none of which seems ideal and many of which leave people feeling powerless, disenfranchised and, in many cases, oppressed and deprived of creative freedom. Surely we could do better than this is the cry arising from many hearts. And when we can't do better, we see a growing sense of disillusionment with, and alienation from, the economic and political forces that control our lives.

For adults of our time, this is an unhappy scene, indeed a deeply disturbing one. Those structures and institutions meant to empower people often hugely disappoint. Even in democratic countries, where people have the right to vote, having exercised that right they then become effectively passive citizens till the next election. In the meantime, governments can, and often do, mitigate or even abandon the very promises on which they were elected. Those with the power always seem to win in the end; those without it begin to see themselves as perpetual losers.

Several complex issues arise here. I will attempt to name and clarify some of the key factors in the hope of providing the context for adults to converse more effectively on issues that impact significantly on their lives and well-being and, as a consequence, stand a better chance of challenging unjust systems and institutions, with a view to exerting some change for the better. In our codependent culture, ignorance seems to be the great enemy, and while access to the Internet makes crucial information readily available to more people, adults still struggle with how to effect systemic change for a better world that would guarantee a more fulfilling life for all.

Inherited Assumptions

Books on political science often begin with the classical Greek period and the theories of Plato and Aristotle. It is a subtle but powerful way to validate current forms of governance and monetary management. At the heart of this classical paradigm is the ruling sky-God who exercises governance downward through key human representatives in their "City of God" on earth. Foremost among such earthly governors is the *king*. In the modern world, kingships have largely been superseded, only to be replaced by presidents, prime ministers, and various types of autocrats whose power and dominance resemble that of a king much more explicitly than most people wish to acknowledge.

This top-down system is derived from a more enduring cultural analogue known as *patriarchy*. Theorists of various disciplines trace its history along different lines, usually within the space of the past five thousand years, and frequently restrict the context to the past two thousand years. I suggest we need a much larger time frame to understand this phenomenon in its full virulence. I trace this most recent wave of patriarchal dominance (previous ones may have existed about which we now know nothing) to the shadow side of the agricultural revolution, an evolutionary emergence that itself is being reconsidered at the present time (see Taylor 2005).

Conventionally, we trace the rise of Agriculture to about ten thousand years ago (c. 8,000 B.C.E.). Humans had been cultivating land and producing food for thousands, possibly millions, of years before then. However, for a range of reasons that have not been clearly delineated, across northern and central Europe (as we now know it), an accelerated wave of land domestication transpired about ten thousand years ago. Rapid growth in human population and the onset of a new Ice Age may have been the primary contributing factors to this new development.

However, the religious validation of this patriarchal upsurge probably belongs to Northern Africa and the Middle East, rather than to the domestication of land in Europe. About eight thousand years ago (c. 6,000 B.C.E.), the freezing conditions reached Northern Africa, causing what today we know as the Sahara desert, stretching eastward to the present-day Arabian desert. Prior to that time both North Africa and the Arabian peninsula were a thriving fertile crescent. The onset of the Ice Age rapidly changed the landscape.

Humans seem to have responded as they had done in Europe. A new aggressive, warrior type male came to the fore. A panic toward greater control became the guiding value. A new aggressiveness emerged, what Steve Taylor (2005, 104ff) describes as an *ego explosion*. And it became progressively more militant and domineering.

To justify and validate the new dispensation, humans engineered a new God concept: a *ruling sky God,* who mandated that humans rule and govern as well. But for reasons that are difficult to discern, it was only some humans who were given that divine right: namely, *males*. Females, and their previous contribution to the development of the earth and its resources, seem to have been rapidly demonized and suppressed. As a species we still seem to be trapped in that subverted genderizing and are still trying to rectify its inherent drive toward female disempowerment and the suppression of feminine qualities in men and women alike.

It is amazing, even scary, how quickly and unquestioningly humans adopt prevailing cultural norms, largely oblivious it seems to how such ideas undermine the ability to live and behave as a more authentic adult. Across the contemporary world, the majority of religious believers embrace the notion of a God who rules from on high, a male governor whose wisdom is percolated downward through a series of male mediators, some angelic and others human.

In the classical cultures of Asia the king came to be seen as the primary representative of God on earth. Kings seem to have evolved for the first time, around 5,000 B.C.E. Prior to that time tribal clan leaders were common, but exercised a level of leadership arising from clan or tribal delegation. Going much further back, we trace the role of the Shaman(ess), with a much more specific religious significance. The tribal chief seems to have had more organizational or practical responsibility while the shaman was the revered spiritual guide within the tribal group.

All that changed with the evolution of the king, whose earthly power and control were in a direct line with that of the God, who ruled from above the sky. God was in the heavens, and kings ruled on God's behalf on earth.

What precisely led to this new arrangement is not at all clear. We witness a stultified cosmic view, an outlook very different from what existed previously for possibly thirty thousand years. Female imagery of the divine, with the Great Mother Goddess as the primary envisaged embodiment of God, was subverted — and progressively demonized as we witness in many of the major world religions we know today.

Finally, Christian faith adopted the prevailing sense of power. Shortly before his death in April 311 C.E., the Roman emperor Gelarius embraced Christianity as the official religion of the Roman empire. His successor, Constantine, fully endorsed the new faith but subjected it totally to his own whim and fancy. This incorporation of Christianity into Roman imperialism drastically changed Gospel Christianity and secularized the fledgling faith into a new imperial system that effectively prevailed until the mid-twentieth century (see Crossan 2007).

For most of that time, kings ruled in Europe and throughout the world. They were honored, even worshiped as divine represen- tatives. The colonial invasions of Latin America, Asia, and Africa imposed regimes heavily influenced by the royal patriarchal faith of the conquering Europeans. The formal adoption of the nation-state at the treaty marking the peace of Westphalia in 1648 gave added impetus to the patriarchal system with its philosophy of divide-and-conquer. Now there was a clearer sense of territorial dominance and responsibility. Although colonialism faded throughout the twentieth century, its influences are still apparent, particularly in deviant forms of internalized oppression as seen in the case of Zimbabwe or Burma, with godlike dictators robbing millions of their potential to become responsible adults, totally controlling people, their land, and their resources.

The baggage of this inherited patriarchal domination is still solidly in place — politically and religiously. On closer investigation, we can see that the system is actually fragmenting, a fact that is consciously concealed by those heavily committed to keeping things as they are. And this is the evidence for the breakdown: those challenging, and especially anybody suggesting an alternative approach, are likely to be ridiculed, demonized, and marginalized. A clear-cut alternative is emerging, born out of a visionary dream of the United Nations in the 1940s, namely, the concept of the NGO (the nongovernmental organization). Today we call it *networking,* and its ascending credibility is evolving much faster than most people realize.

The Controlling Power of Money

Before exploring the culture of networking in our time and its ability to evoke more adult ways of living and behaving, the political background depicted above needs to be supplemented with some considerations on how we use, and abuse, money. People feel disempowered by how political governance operates, and within that entrapment is the crucial issue of money, the inordinate influence it has on all our lives, and the widespread political trend to camouflage financial truth so that people will not (and often cannot) ask for adult accountability.[14]

Paul Hawken makes this perceptive remark: "Money and economics are among the most talked about and least understood facets of human civilization. Just as most people speak without giving a lot of thought to what they say, most of us open our wallets in the same way" (online interview: *www.worldchanging.com/archives/007310.html*). And David C. Korten (2006, 138), himself once a business tycoon, sounds an even more alarmist note: "The rule of money works all the better for corporate plutocrats because most people are wholly unaware of the ways in which the organizing principles of Empire have become embedded in the money system."

Both Hawken and Korten expose one of the most serious flaws in contemporary culture: codependency is far more rampant and deep-seated than we suspect. Millions of people have abdicated their adult sense of responsibility, entrusting to major institutions — in this case, financial ones — concerns that the people themselves should be managing and directing. In many cases we don't know what is going on — about the very things that impinge upon our daily lives — and in some cases, we don't want to know. This is *not* being adult, no matter how we define the term; on reflection it is grossly infantile. While we choose to keep our heads buried in the quicksands of cultural ignorance, then indeed we weave a web of alienation and disempowerment that can be immensely destructive. We need to change and do so urgently — and the first major step in that conversion is the wake-up call to become more aware of what is actually happening in our world.

Bernard Lietaer (2001) provides valuable insight into the evolution of money, its empowering function, and the gradual erosion of its cultural significance. There are many web pages that make money and its complexities more accessible to the average citizen. And a little history is also helpful. With the nation-state becoming the official unit for governance in Europe in 1648, the concept of national banks evolved for the first time. Yet money did not become legal tender until 1668 (in Sweden). For long, money was a mechanism used in gift-exchange, with fluid value to be determined by those doing the exchanging. As the industrial revolution happened in Britain, money as payment for labor came to the fore and formal banking was introduced in 1694.[15]

With the publication of Adam Smith's *The Wealth of Nations* in 1776, the science of modern economics was born. *Scarcity* became the new economic principle and remains so to the present day. In an influential 1932 essay, Lionel Robbins defined economics as "the science which studies human behavior as a relationship between ends and scarce means which have alternative uses." The concept of *scarcity* became a foundational element in our understanding of economics. A resource is considered scarce when its availability is not enough to meet its demand. Scarcity is based on the idea that oftentimes a limited supply of goods or services comes up against an ever increasing demand for it and that, as such, every effort must be made to ensure its proper utilization and distribution so as to avoid inefficiency. Most goods and services can be defined as scarce since individuals desire more of them than they already possess (scarcity is maintained by demand). Those that are readily abundant are referred to as free goods. This must be one of the best kept secrets of all time: pragmatically attractive, but spiritually disastrous.

The principle of *scarcity* became the rationale and justification for fierce competition, an open playing field in which the "invisible hand" of the market will assure the best and most productive outcome. Here the market is assigned semi-divine status. The political divine right has now seeped from politics into economics. Today they still function hand-in-glove. And the consequent brutality of the system, leaving most of humanity impoverished for most of the time, and the earth's resources usurped, exploited, and consumed to the advantage of the rich and powerful, is postulated as a necessary outcome for an efficient economic system. Efficient for those consumed by self-interest, but certainly not congenial to adult wisdom, nor can it be considered to be spiritually or ethically sustainable in any serious sense.

The prodigious and fertile creation is deviously slighted, and grossly misconstrued in order to justify a flawed economic theory. The basic principle of God's creation is *abundance,* not *scarcity.* There are abundant resources on earth to sustain and nourish the entire web of life — including the feeding of the human population — provided the resources are accessed and used in an equitable, just, and sustainable fashion. Instead of neo-classical economics we need what Sallie McFague (2001, 100ff) calls *ecological economics:*

The big picture is lost; it is as if the human economy takes place in a vacuum, in isolation from any setting, any limits, any laws other than its own. Hence, the difference of "who we are" in these two economic paradigms is striking: the one (neo-classical) begins with individual human beings and their desire for material goods, while the other (ecological) with human beings as a species, a very needy one, dependent on a complex but vulnerable living space. The first view says we are consumers of nature's wealth; the other view, that we are members of nature's household.

Today, most of the earth's resources (the household) are in the hands, not of national governments, but of transnational corporations. Under the approval and protection of WTO law, corporations gain access to resources not even located within their own geographical jurisdiction. Even human body fluids and tissue have been patented by megacorporations, a process in which national governments are totally helpless. Corporations rule the modern world and hold most of the wealth. They know no scarcity but very effectively exploit the earth and its peoples in the name of an economic theory of scarcity.

An economics based on the law of scarcity is a blatant lie. Its veracity is not in what it stipulates but in its capacity to favor the powerful, who dominate and control while simultaneously relegating to poverty and codependence the weak and vulnerable. The entire capitalistic system is rotten at the core.

Proponents claim that despite its limitations it is still the best system, since we have not come up with anything better. By their very nature, patriarchal systems are self-perpetuating; they cannot, and will not, entertain any serious alternatives. "Socialism" has become the label for all other alternatives and is readily demonized by those who hold the power. In the opening decade of the twentieth century a worldwide economic recession exposed gross exploitation by banking institutions and reckless financiers. These were unambiguous signals of a system that could easily implode under the weight of its own corruption. After numerous bailouts by mainline governments, a measure of normality was restored, but it is obvious to many that the capitalistic system is in a fragile state and cannot be sustained indefinitely.

Other economic models are known, and some have been tried out on a small scale (see Lietaer 2001; Cavanagh 2002). They employ principles of subsidiarity and sustainability, and they do work. They return power to the people, prioritize local endeavor, safeguard good ecological practice, use imagination and creativity in relating to, and using, the gifts of the living earth. And such endeavors tend to be supported by an empowering spiritual consciousness.

Money for long was regarded as a spiritual resource to reinforce a culture of mutual giftedness. It was certainly not an economic utopia, but offered a great deal more hope and justice than our contemporary capitalistic model. There are alternative models we can adopt, and sooner than we think we may be obliged to take that unprecedented step.

Quantum Theory and the Birth of Networking

Our mainstream political and economic structures, like our religious ones, are becoming increasingly cumbersome, bureaucratic, and irrelevant. In a word, they have largely outlived their usefulness. As we move into a more conscious sense of being coevolutionary adults, the rhetoric of patriarchal governance exerts a diminishing sense of appeal and a stronger sense of irrelevance. We see no cogent reasons for investing energy in that which seems alien to our deeper aspirations. Correspondingly, we find ourselves drawn to other ways of being and other ways of engaging with our world. As we move into the twenty-first century, one structure in particular exerts a growing attraction for protean adults: *networking*. It has more in its favor than initially meets the eye.

Networking can be seen as a by-product of quantum physics. It manifests that kind of wholeness captivated in the notion that *the whole is greater than the sum of the parts*. Contrary to most of the institutions we know so well, networks don't operate out of a cause-and-effect dynamic; they embody a fluidity and flexibility that cannot be entertained in most institutions; they thrive on relationality rather than on hierarchical domination. They are open to surprise and innovation, providing a thriving ground for the more creative adults of our time. In the words of Margaret J. Wheatley (1992, 43– 44):

> My growing sensibility of a quantum universe has affected my organizational life in several ways. First, I try hard to discipline myself to remain aware of the whole and to resist my well-trained desire to analyze the parts to death. I look now for patterns of movement over time and focus on qualities like rhythm, flow, direction, and shape. Second, I know I am wasting time whenever I draw straight arrows between two variables in a cause-and-effect diagram, or position things as polarities, or create elaborate plans and time lines. Third, I no longer argue with anyone about what is real. Fourth, the time I formerly spent on detailed planning and analysis I now use to look at the structures that might facilitate relationships. I have come to expect that something useful occurs if I link up people, units, or tasks, even though I cannot determine precise outcomes. And last, I realize more and more that the universe will not cooperate with my desires for determinism.

Paul Hawken (2007) provides one of the more accessible overviews of how networking functions in the modern world. As we enter the twenty-first century two distinctive developments evoke our attention. First, we are confronted with systemic problems of a global nature (global warming, poverty, violence, etc.), which can no longer be resolved by individual governments acting in isolation and in some cases seem resistant to formal governments acting collaboratively (e.g., the war on terror). Second, we see a worldwide movement of small groups determined to heal the wounds of the earth with the force of passion, dedication, and indigenous wisdom; across the planet, groups ranging from ad hoc neighborhood associations to well-funded international organizations are confronting issues like the destruction of the environment, the abuses of free market capitalism, social justice, and the loss of indigenous cultures.

These two parallel movements converge in a strangely unexpected way. The latter culture of networking has become the conscience that pushes formal governments into urgent action. And this has been the case throughout the closing decades of the twentieth century — right up to the present time. Issues like the hole in the ozone layer, deforestation, biodiversity, threatened species, and, laterally, global warming only became issues of governmental concern — nationally and internationally — when the alarming evidence provided by networks like Greenpeace, Friends of the Earth, Worldwatch, and local ecology groups could no longer be ignored. Sadly, the media tend to highlight governmental response to these crises but rarely give credit to those who forced governments into facing the harsh truth in the first place.

Globalization marks a similar trend with another disastrous outcome. Megacorporations control the finances and material resources of the planet and usurp them, primarily to their own advantage. They also control the large media networks, disseminating information that favors their own advancement but rarely tells the whole truth. Money rules and money controls in economic globalization.

There is an alternative form known as *evolutionary globalization* (see Anderson 2004), initially hailed by Marshall McLuhan's global village in the 1960s. This marks the coming together of the world's peoples — those women and men who constitute the human family, many living in dire poverty and social marginalization, disenfranchised economically and politically. "For this latter group, 'democratic capitalism,' 'economic democracy,' and 'market populism,' are all the same oxymoron" (Hawken 2007, 124). Local endeavors, offering practical help, social empowerment, and some sense of hope in the future exert appeal for those disenfranchised and deprived. It may be some time yet before these diverse and amorphous groups begin a *networking of the networks*. Then the counterrevolution is likely to become much more visible — and culturally more credible.

The human body flourishes through the creative interaction of our cellular make-up. So too with the earth body if it is to enjoy true health (see Capra 2002, 8ff). If the head/brain (read: governance from the top down) seeks to rule over and above the rest of the body then imbalance and sickness will ensue. The evolution of networking in our time may be seen as a wake-up call from the self-organizing (autopoietic) earth-body. The body is sick and suffering, and those in charge are not responding appropriately.

As indicated in previous chapters, the United Nations developed the concept of the NGO in 1945 as a means of including movements and organizations other than formal governments. I wish to suggest there was also a subconscious, underlying motivation: the UN was envisaging the eventual depletion of all patriarchal governance and this would require other means of governance that would honor people's hopes and aspirations. Mainline governments may have suspected this prophetic move and quickly sought to tame and subdue the new networks, sometimes almost to the point of oblivion. However, the concept never faded entirely and is now revisiting our earth with a timely vengeance.

Although many governments collaborate with networks (covertly for the greater part) and in many parts of the world, local governance tends to follow the networking philosophy of fluidity, flexibility, and maximum participation, the power of networking is subverted for the greater part. It has little or no place in formal educational programs other than in multimedia studies. And millions of people, still deluded by the lure of glamor and power, are unaware of this major cultural transition. With the increasing awareness of the challenge to more authentic adulthood, the trend toward networking is likely to hold out enormous hope, with prospects of a more empowering and grace-filled future.

Networking in the Information Age

The World Wide Web connects across time zones and cultures. And it connects primarily through information — in what Daniel Pink (2008) describes as the *Conceptual Age*. Millions readily access information on a whole range of different subjects; this can be both empowering and also overwhelming. And the information channels target new ways for connecting, relating, participating, and collaborating in endeavors of different types. This new participative landscape is the domain of networking.

Involvement in networking can at times be tedious, chaotic, and frustrating. And when the network works, the sense of satisfaction can be exhilarating. In either case, information is the primary stuff being negotiated. This often involves a steep learning curve, and in this new landscape we never cease learning. Networking flourishes on a philosophy of life that is considerably different from mainstream culture, where some provide the knowledge and skill while most remain passive observers. In good networking distinctions between elite and rank-and-file break down. Mutuality, participation, and collaboration provide the modus operandi. And the shift in awareness — the new consciousness — is crucial.

Networks thrive on the principle of: "the whole is greater than the sum of the parts." The power of networking cannot be explained by cause-and-effect dynamics. Rational analysis and hierarchical structures make little sense in this new dispensation. Innovation, trial-and-error, and teamwork are skills for progress. Fluidity, flexibility, and responsiveness to real need are core values. It is a different way of doing that leads to a different way of being.

Fritjof Capra (2002, 94) provides a useful overview for the reflections of this chapter:

> With the new information and communication technologies, social networks have become all-pervasive, both within and beyond organizations. For an organization to be alive, however, the existence of social networks is not sufficient; they need to be networks of a special type. Living networks are self-generating. Each communication creates thoughts and meaning, which give rise to further communication. In this way, the entire network generates itself, producing a common context of meaning, shared knowledge, rules of conduct, a boundary, and a collective identity for its members.

Not for those for whom the hierarchical structure is important, who thrive best under a chain of command and like to know where the buck stops. Coevolving adults cannot flourish in such an environment. And yet we cannot simply shift from one paradigm to another. This is a quantum leap — and it can be risky! But as adults of the twenty-first century do we have any other choice?

(a) **Conventional inherited wisdom** *deems most humans as passive recipients of a guiding power reserved to the enlightened few entrusted with governance characterized by the key values of the patriarchal will to power. In this model empowerment belongs to those who hold and control the power.*

(b) **Embedded codependency** *results in the majority being disempowered, often to the point of infantilism, ultimately a breeding ground for cynicism, apathy, and destructive violence.*

(c) **Adult empowerment** *requires a re-visioning of what empowering structures might look like where adults in particular can become involved with greater mutuality and participation. Networking seems to be an evolving model to meet this need.*

Chapter Fourteen

Doing Ritual in an Adult Way

FOCUS: For most Christian people ritual translates into liturgy and sacrament, with a distinctive assignment to who can facilitate the ceremony. As people mature into a more adult sense of faith they begin to realize that ritual-making is everybody's prerogative, and everybody's responsibility.

Imitation can be deadly, even if it is imitation of Christ.
— GUS GORDON

For Mina Meinhoffer, nursing was a saving grace. Subconsciously, she had probably opted for a nursing career in order to nurse the sick, hurt child within herself. That became more apparent as she struggled to make sense of her own children: their births, their transitions, and their coming into adult maturity.

It was Melissa's eleventh birthday. She was the eldest daughter, a beautiful handsome girl rapidly approaching puberty. Mina, her mother, felt a huge sense of responsibility. She did not want Melissa to go through the torture of mind and soul she herself had to endure as a teenager. It was not so much the lack of information as the bequeathing of mis-information. Her coming of age was shrouded in dark mystery with each menstrual cycle carrying the possibility that she could bleed to death, the designated affliction because she was a daughter of Eve! For Mina those teenage years retained a painful memory, and were it not for her career in nursing, they might well haunt her to this day.

One day, Melissa came home early from school; she had not been feeling well. "Well, my love," explained Mina, "it is that stage in your life when changes might be happening in your body, and per-haps that's the reason you feel poorly." "What changes, Mum?" The conversation took off from there, and what a precious experience it was for both mother and daughter. One of those memorable moments when heart connects with heart.

For long, Mina had a fantasy that young women should celebrate their first menstrual period as one might celebrate a birthday or a special occasion. After all, she reasoned, it is probably one of the most significant experiences a young woman will ever know. Its implications are enormous and presumably blessed by God. So why not celebrate? She talked to Melissa about this and the ongoing conversation began to engage some of her school friends. Some were thrilled; others were scared. One parent objected strongly and reported her concern to the head teacher; another, in moral indignation, went to the local priest, while the evangelically minded Mrs. Blanhufler was disgusted that such an idea was afloat and threatened to report Mina to the police.

But the party took place: five young teenagers, their mothers and two of the fathers gathered to celebrate. And what an amazing party! It turned out to be a ritual, with an anointing with clay tinged with the girls' menstrual blood (all the girls were asked to keep this a secret), each mother prayed a lengthy blessing and in the process laid hands on the five initiates. They sang a few simple chants and ended together in prayer.

Initially, they considered inviting the local pastor, but his nega-tive and denunciatory response, based upon one parent's complaint, nearly scuppered the whole endeavor. It takes courage to proceed after the wisdom from on high has denounced you!

L ATE INTO THE EVENING the group talked and laughed, shared and prayed, danced and celebrated. The purpose was to ensure that the young women would feel good about their bodies and about all that was transpiring around their puberty and adolescence. The involved parents wanted to reassure them of their love and support, affirmation and encouragement. What a wonderful intro-duction to their adolescent years! More significantly, what a powerful illustration of the human capacity for ritual-making!

People of Ritual

This story illustrates one simple but profound fact: we all have within us the capacity for ritual. We do not need to employ a specially designated person to do it for us. There is no magic to it, other than the sheer magic that emanates from its performance. And what an amazing sense of empowerment — for everybody involved, not least for the adults who initiated and facilitated the ritual experience.

How did we learn to do ritual? We have known it intuitively from time immemorial. Perhaps we learned it from the other creatures with whom we share the planet: the animals, the birds, the fishes. They all perform ritual acts, whether driven by instinct or desire. The difference is that while the animals follow fixed, repeated patterns, we humans can cocreate as we go along.

We don't have to be overly preoccupied about defining what exactly we mean by ritual. In a sense, history provides its own answer. As far back as six hundred thousand years ago, when our ancient ancestors gathered around the newly discovered sense of fire, already at the preverbal stage of human communication, they had a cumulative sense of the mystery that surrounded them, and they acknowledged it by dancing around the fire. This was ritual behavior, honoring and worshiping the spirit of fire, the Spirit of the living earth itself.

Much closer to our own time, in the region of a hundred thousand years ago, we humans buried our dead with some quite elaborate rituals. We believed we were still in contact with the dead and that we could enhance their journey to the afterlife by blessing the dead body with ochre clay, fruits, and various emblems dear to the departed one. And we commended the dead to the universal forces that held the secrets of life and death. In these ritual enactments we made profound and powerful statements about our belief in the divine, the immanence of the divine with us, and the continuation of life after the experience of death.

As we move into the Palaeolithic Era, we encounter the elaborately symbolic world of Ice Age art, which may well have been motivated by the desire for ritual expression, with the cave as a center for ritualistic celebration. Initially dated back to about forty thousand years ago, our human ability to create artistically has taken something of a quantum leap in recent years. We know that our ancient ancestors in Ethiopia as far back as 2.2 million years ago were creating stone artifacts that were original and elegant by the standard of those times. The discovery of the Blombos Caves in Lesotho in 1991 pushed back the formal dates for artistic engagement to about 100,000 years ago. And then in 2008 came the spectacular discoveries of Pinnacle Point in South Africa, which have been dated to 164,000 years ago.

Already at this stage we have moved beyond ritual for ritual's sake. We are into a new stage of ritual development, which today we call *rites of passage*. The burial customs of some hundred thousand years ago had already evolved into rites of passage. Such rites are universally associated with major life transitions, such as birth, death, and developmental stages such as puberty and menarche. But perhaps the better known rites of passage belong to the seasonal changes of nature marking the first rains, the solstice, the season for sowing, the time for reaping.

All life was perceived as a cycle of divine birthing. Every transition was noted and celebrated, presumably with a wide range of ritual across different landscapes and tribal groups. Scholars often suggest that it was fear more than anything else that motivated such ritualistic behavior. The argument tends to go along these lines: gripped in the ignorance and superstition of ancient times, people were at the mercy of their own irrational projections. Progressively they became civilized and enlightened, and as they did so, they abandoned their archaic beliefs and practices. Scholars then go on to postulate that the peoples of today's "undeveloped" nations still need to shed this baggage from the past.

One wonders who is doing the projecting: our ancient ancestors or the cultural barbarians of our so-called developed world? As indicated previously, I do not wish to glamorize the past nor romanticize about our ancient ancestors. They certainly did not get it all right, and for the greater part, we do not have concrete objective evidence with which to assess and evaluate what they were up to. But we do have tentative evidence, and with today's sophisticated technology we are rapidly filling gaps in our knowledge. The growing body of research is not verifying the existence of an ancient savage, cannibalistic or noble, but rather of an earth creature, enlightened and spiritually sensitive, precisely because that creature remained so close to the earth and its life cycles. And it is from within the earth-connectedness that the capacity for ritual flourishes across ancient times and cultures.

American Catholic missionary Vincent J. Donovan, C.S.Sp., went to work with the Masai people of Kenya in the 1960s and 1970s. Contrary to many of his age he did not go to Africa to convert the pagan peoples. He went with the conviction that God would be there before him. Therefore, his first task was to be a recipient: by observing and listening to the indigenous people and their culture. He was particularly fascinated by their rituals and their enormous potential to create highly ornate ceremonies and rites of passage. In time it became apparent that the seven sacraments of the Catholic Church, which he was missioned to bring, were already there in embryonic form, and in some cases, expressed in a depth of ritual meaning far more engaging than the conventional Catholic modes of celebration. The fruit of his discovery is explored in his book *The Church in the Midst of Creation* (Donovan 1989).

This story illustrates three developmental stages in the evolution of ritual celebration. First, there is the innate capacity for ritual that all humans exhibit especially in social behavior. Various gestures of greeting: handshakes, bowing, hugging, kissing, saluting — all embody ritual intent. Collective celebrations such as birthdays, marriages, carnivals are social expressions of the same basic orientation. It seems to me that every piece of ritualistic behavior, no matter how secular or convoluted, has spiritual intent (at the subconscious level). All ritual carries a deep unspeakable desire for connection, relationship, meaning, even for transcendence. Strictly speaking there is no such thing as purely secular ritual.

Second, in every culture, ancient and modern, we inadvertently translate our need for ritual into communal celebrations, which then assume the significance of rites of passage. Every culture tends to have ceremonies marking birth and death, but also significant life experiences such as marriage, anniversaries, work changes, moving to a new home. Even in our modern cultures, where the institution of marriage is in deep crisis, people still formalize their commitment and seek to nourish it with special celebrations.

Much more significant, and problematic for our time, are the compensatory forms of ritual celebration. Because the formal channels for such celebrations (via the religions) have become problematic for many people today, we now inadvertently act out our need for ritual in a wide range of misplaced or deviant behaviors. For the younger generation, the disco has become a major focus for ritual enactment with the ecstasy of rapidly beating music, glaring lights, and stimulating drugs. In the adult world, party-going has assumed a cult of transcendence often involving sexual behavior, use of drugs, and consumption of alcohol. Body exercise, especially body building and shaping, has assumed ritual potency in many Western nations.

Bruce Wilshire (1998) offers an intriguing study in which he suggests that the proliferation of addictive behaviors today corresponds to the primal hunger we are suffering, precisely because we don't have healthy ecstatic outlets for our creativity. Our compulsions are distorted expressions of our need for ritual. Some modern theorists suggest that the current increase in addictive behavior is correlated quite closely with our distance from nature and our lack of facility to be nursed by nature's healing and restoring powers.

Sacramental Experience

All of this brings me to the third layer of ritual enactment: *sacramentality*. This is a distinctively religious term, one that belongs mainly to the Christian religions. In the Christian understanding, sacraments provide special occasions when we experience the closeness of God through our participation in a sacramental service. Baptism and Eucharist (Communion) are the two sacraments most widely adopted in the different Christian churches. The former is a once-only event, marking the initiation of a new member into a particular denomination while also providing something akin to a consecration of the child or young person to God. Eucharist, on the other hand, is a regular weekly or daily event.

Sacraments like baptism, confirmation, marriage, and the anointing of the sick (or dying) all mark significant life stages. These do not originate with one or another religion. They imitate quite closely the rites of passage known universally over thousands of years. Situated explicitly in a church context, they come to be regarded as an aspect of the formal religion, and correspondingly their cultural, social, and personal meaning is often obscured or subverted. Instead of being human experiences that touch deeper layers of meaning, they are often construed as proof for the existence of God. In our unenlightened desire to protect God — arising from our failure to develop a more adult sense of faith — we end up promoting neither the reality of God nor the spiritual well being of the human.

By absorbing the need for ritual into the formal religious context we are in danger of disempowering people of their innate capacity for ritual. We attribute great significance to the celebration of a marriage, irrespective of whether there is a religious ceremony or not. I suggest that if formal religion did not provide the ceremony, the people themselves would almost certainly create marriage celebrations of a distinctively religious nature.

Secular funerals have become quite popular in modern Europe. They tend to be carried out with dignity and sensitivity and genuinely celebrate the life of the departed one with a ritual repertoire that probably would not be accepted in some public places of worship. However, one also detects in these rituals a lack of familiar boundaries whereby people's need to grieve is not adequately catered to. Good ritual at times requires a sense of continuity with tradition.

An important point to note here is that no person or group, no matter how uncaring, will simply dispose of a dead relative devoid of all ritual celebration. Instinctively, we know that the end of life has meaning and significance and needs to be marked with some sense of public honor. And in the absence of somebody equipped with the wisdom for ritual enactment, one or more people will volunteer to lead a prayer, a tribute, a service, etc. Indeed, it is often in the face of crisis or catastrophe that our capacity for ritual becomes most apparent. In the U.K. we witnessed this on a national scale in the aftermath of the death of Diana, princess of Wales, in September 1997.

Ritualizing the Gift of Food

The Eucharist is a particularly well known ritual, celebrated in one form or another in every major religion known to humankind. In the Christian rendition, the understanding is that the elements of bread and wine are changed in some unique and mysterious way, through the special power of the priest. Theologically, our understanding of Eucharist is quite complex. Not only is it a context in which we communicate with God through the nourishment of the proclaimed scripture and the reception of Holy Communion, but we also celebrate symbolically the saving death of Jesus. Some scholars understand the Eucharist to be a symbolic reenactment of Calvary whereby Jesus once more gives of his body and blood for the salvation of people.

Several motifs are invoked in this understanding of Eucharist, and one wonders if they enhance or diminish the significance of Eucharist as a ritual celebration. Some Christian churches attribute great importance to the fact that each Eucharist emulates what happened in the Upper Room on the night before Jesus died. On the assumption that only the male apostles participated in this special event (the Last Supper), some churches go on to argue that only males can preside at Eucharistic celebrations in today's church. In such arguments, I suggest, we have largely lost the Eucharist as a ritual act and got entangled in ecclesiastical power games.

In its primordial meaning Eucharist is *a celebration of food*. It serves as a continual reminder that all food is gift, to be received with gratitude and joy, that in the giftedness of food we experience something of God's own gracious immediacy to us. This, I suspect, is a very ancient conviction: God comes close to the people in a unique way in the sharing and eating of food. All food is sacred. All food is closely associated with the nourishing power of the divine. Therefore, over time we have evolved special sacred meals (such as Eucharist) to provide a context to express our gratitude and to know, in a more real way, God's closeness to us.

In terms of primordial meaning, every Eucharist is first and foremost *a sacred meal*. Traditional Catholics tend to emphasize the "sacrifice of the Mass," associating the Eucharist with the death of

Jesus. I leave it to theologians to justify this interpretation, but as a social scientist, I am left wondering if it does not obfuscate the more basic meaning of Eucharist long known to the human family. Might this not be another example where the preoccupations of formal religion distract from more ancient spiritual meaning!

The ritual significance of Eucharist has certainly been undermined by the close link with formal priesthood (male or female). Christian cultures carry a widespread assumption that it is through the power of the priest that the elements of bread and wine are converted into sacred food. The more we project an image of the empowered priest the more we are implicitly invoking the idea of a disempowered people.

When we look closely at the prayer structure of Eucharistic celebrations, we see that those based on informed theology state quite explicitly that the agent for change is not the priest but the Holy Spirit. In Eucharistic theology, the *epiclesis* (invocation of the Holy Spirit) is a crucial element in Eucharistic liturgies. In fact, there is usually a double invocation: before the consecration invoking the Holy Spirit to transform the bread and wine into the body and blood of Christ; and after the consecration, the Holy Spirit is invoked to touch the hearts of those about to receive the gifts so that they too will be renewed through the power of what they receive. (In some traditions, the two invocations are combined as one; see Crockett 1989.)

The problem being highlighted here is not just a Christian one. In some African tribes and among indigenous peoples around the world, ceremonies for rites of passage tend to be facilitated by male leaders and rarely by females, even in reference to female members of the group. What we are encountering here is the invasive and distorting influence of patriarchy, seriously distracting from the deeper meaning of the ritual, but also desecrating the ritual itself by making it the prerogative of special people, of powerful role, but not necessarily of holy disposition.

The Adult as Ritual Maker

I opened this chapter with a vivid illustration of an adult person engaging other adults in activating a ritual celebration — for pubescent young females. Mrs. Meinhoffer did not seek permission from any religious authority, she did not use any prescribed texts, nor did she feel any need to follow official procedures, sacred or secular. And yet the ritual was clearly endowed with spiritual meaning. For Mina Meinhoffer, female puberty was a special moment that needed to be celebrated in a joyous and sacred way.

A great deal of ritual responsibility rests with each one of us becoming more aware of the human need for good ritual, of the responsibility for each person to take desired initiatives, for the courage and the wisdom to challenge unhealthy fear and caution, particularly from those who claim a religious or ecclesiastical monopoly. However, we are dealing with a process that can invoke deep emotion and various degrees of spirit power. Consequently, ritual development always needs to evolve within a dialogical context, so that appropriate discernment can take place on what procedures should be adopted and what safety guidelines need to be put in place.

Official liturgists strongly emphasize tradition as the guardian of more authentic ritual. Tradition in itself is no guarantee of truth or reliability. Tradition can often be locked into particular past expressions and procedures that may have outgrown their usefulness and therefore can be barriers rather than assets for spiritual empowerment. Ideally, good ritual invokes inherited wisdom but strives to translate it into contemporary context and expression in order to serve contemporary need. Once again, communal dialogue rather than isolated initiative is not merely a discerning safety valve, but also can provide the mobilization of diverse giftedness so necessary for ritual enrichment.

Returning to the focus of the present work on adult faith development, I would like to conclude the present chapter by revisiting the prophetic adult stance of Mina Meinhoffer. Paradoxically her creativity is born out of personal dysfunctionality, which left her with a great deal of pain and soul searching. Many searching adults today will resonate with such experience. However, her true adult self is revealed in the courage and wisdom of her transformative grace, and its liberating power not merely for herself and for her daughter, but for the many others who were touched, directly and indirectly, by her creative response. I highlight three salient factors:

1. Mina is painfully aware of her dysfunctional background in terms of her own adolescent awakening, and this evokes her creative urge to handle her daughter's puberty differently. As far as we can detect, Mina is not wallowing in her inherited pain, nor is she merely projecting it onto her daughter. Instead of playing the victim of her painful past, she transforms it into a creative response for her daughter's current situation. In that way she liberates and empowers her daughter while also healing and empowering something deep within herself.

Millions of people in the contemporary world are caught in the vicious web of *victimization*. Even people who bring their deep wounds into therapy can take quite a long time to outgrow the victim role. A sense of victimization can be grounded in legitimate hurt accrued in the past, but rehearsing it continuously, or seeking out scapegoats to blame, rarely resolves the issue and can keep a person trapped in a type of codependency that makes the evolution of genuine adulthood difficult if not totally impossible. For the adult to come forth, the attention-seeking prop of the victim has to be transcended.

The transcendence of the victim basically means shifting the focus to the status of a *survivor:* I am no longer a victim but a survivor. It is from this more adult stance that I can begin to become proactive in calling forth the adult in others as Mina does with her daughter and the other adults she engaged in the ritual.

2. Mina addresses her concern for her daughter with creativity, intuition, imagination, and courage. These are adult qualities not always promoted in our formal culture and often subverted because of the perceived threat they pose. She obviously talked to her daughter and discussed issues with her. Intuitively, however, she knows that ritualization is an aid to integration far deeper than any advice or verbal encouragement.

In this process she is taking risks, particularly in the contemporary culture where the issue of child abuse evokes alarmist concern; she could easily be reported to state authorities. The likelihood of rebuff from religious authorities is even higher, as they may feel that she is transgressing into their territory, attempting something that should be the reserve of pastoral care under the guidance and supervision of those competently trained. Her engagement with other parents provided the dialogical context that helps to offset negative reaction; more importantly it provides the impetus for her prophetic courage and wisdom.

3. By engaging and involving other parents — in a sensitive and responsible way — Mina exhibits another important feature of our evolving sense of the adult. This is a different quality of adulthood from society's cherished role of the robust individual, the lone ranger who is assumed to know it all and need not be dependent on anybody else. Mina is a collaborator, a teamworker. Quite likely she is one of those people who learns as she goes along and cherishes the added insights and modifications that dialogue with significant others provides.

This also protects her against the allegations of being some type of New Age freak, or one influenced by the latest pop theories of child development. She is not looking over her shoulder for fear of higher authorities (codependent behavior), but is exercising a creative empowering form of adult mutuality and in that process empowering other people to lay claim to their authentic adult-selves.

(a) **Conventional inherited wisdom** *overidentifies ritual with liturgy and ecclesiastical sacraments, requiring the specialized skills of minister or liturgist, continually reminding lay participants that they are merely passive recipients.*

(b) **Embedded codependency** *begets unworthiness, inferiority, and a ritual kind of mystique that placates and pacifies, but rarely empowers in an authentic adult way.*

(c) **Adult empowerment** *highlights the fact that empowering ritual is an innate capacity of every human, translated religiously into rites and sacraments, which need to be celebrated in a way in which adult people know they are participating in a transformative, empowering, and sacred experience.*

Chapter Fifteen

When Adults Die Gracefully

FOCUS: From our patriarchal culture we have inherited an understanding that loss, letting go, and death are weaknesses to be fought against, limitations to be overcome. Adults, more at home in a creation endowed with paradox, are challenged to befriend loss and to let go in a different, more integrated way.

I anticipate that most of what we call religion today will die in the next century. Rigor mortis has already set in. Out of that death, however, will come a new beginning. I am glad that I have lived to see the birth pangs. — JOHN SHELBY SPONG

On the outside it looked like a shed, perhaps a storage place for a range of objects worth keeping, although they would never be used again. Officially it was a mortuary, where dead bodies were stored until burial could be arranged. Now it was stacked to the roof with corpses, people who had died of HIV/AIDS. Keeping the stench of body-decay within the galvanized structure had become impossible. And most of the bodies would not be claimed, because either there was no family member left to claim them, or an already impoverished people could not get around to burying their dead. And those delegated with the task of mass burials had also run out of burial space, time, and money.

THE LEGACY OF some primitive, barbaric culture? An exaggerated tale that could never happen! I actually witnessed it personally — and the experience will haunt me for the rest of my life. It was the month of May 2004, the country in question being Zambia in East

Africa. And I suspect the grotesque scene was replicated in many other poor countries — in Africa and beyond.

Our Death-Ridden World

An adult way of dealing with death is virtually unknown in the modern world. Millions die each day due to poverty, disease, violence, neglect, and warfare. And millions are not buried with respect or dignity; many end up in mass graves or are left to decay in total abandonment. In our modern world, abandonment is the plight of most of those who die.

In the developed countries, we bury our dead with a lot of formal, sometimes morbid, ritual, and then we quickly forget about those who have departed. We deal with death in a very contained and controlled way. It helps to keep emotion subject to reason and keeps us safe from having to deal with our vulnerability and immortality. Engaging with death in an adult way is largely unknown in the modern world. Charles A. Corr (2008) provides a useful overview of how a range of different cultures deal with death and dying. Even where elaborate and creative rituals are adopted, death is still experienced as a frightening malicious curse, rather than a life transition inherently necessary for evolutionary growth and development.

The Christian religion adopts a strangely paradoxical way of dealing with death. Death is an evil to be superseded in a life hereafter, a kind of curse consequent upon the flaw of original sin, an anomaly that hopefully we will get rid of someday. However, according to the Christian faith, there is the consolation of knowing that we will live forever after death, so the immortality that we cannot achieve in this life, at least we'll have the satisfaction of knowing it in the next.

This issue of immortality is a central tenet of Christian faith, above and beyond any other major religious system. Echoes of patriarchal power rumble in the background, making it inconceivable that dominant humans might have to face the same demise as everything else in God's creation. To become compost for new life just is not good enough for ruling superior beings, so they postulate the possibility of living forever.

It is this eternal addiction that inhibits humans in coming to terms with death in a more realistic and responsible way. And the massive denial that accompanies death, in turn, impacts upon our engagement with life. Life and death belong integrally to the cycle of birth–death–rebirth. They are intimately intertwined, and a depraved engagement with the one seriously impacts upon the other.

Reclaiming a More Adult Approach

We tend not to talk about death, and we avoid thinking about it as much as possible. Philosophically and religiously, we speculate about it, relegating its meaning to a world beyond, thus leaving us with a human and earthly calamity consigned to the shadows of denial. Humans urgently need to develop a strategy to deal with death in a more responsibly adult way, to dialogue about its meaning, and converse about our feelings and values in dealing with it. I hope the brief reflections of this chapter will assist in that process.

First, death is an integral dimension of all life forms, from the great cosmic realm to the microorganisms that underpin the web of life. As already indicated in chapter 11 above, the paradox of creation-and-destruction, or the cycle of birth–death–rebirth, pervades the entire spectrum of creation. Death is an essential ingredient in this life-giving process. Death seems to be a prerequisite for new birth and reanimated life. It is not a flaw to be rectified or some curse from which humanity needs to be rescued.

Patriarchal cultures cannot tolerate paradoxes. One cannot control a paradox, and in the patriarchal consciousness anything that cannot be controlled is in danger of being out of control. If something is out of (human) control then the patriarchal will to power is not totally in charge. Hence the Christian (patriarchal) claim that death is the last enemy to be conquered. Christians postulate that this has happened through the death and resurrection of Jesus, yet Christianity is among the most death-inflicting systems in the world. The theory has not been translated into reality. Perhaps it can't be, because it is essentially false to begin with.

In adult faith, we see death as a divinely bestowed endowment — paradoxical, yet divinely endowed. It is not an evil, but something fundamentally good. It is not a deviant force to be conquered and eliminated, but rather a paradoxical life force awaiting our befriending compliance. From a human point of view it does not, and in my opinion, never will, make full sense to human beings, a dilemma Charles Foster (2009) embraces with admirable courage and wisdom. Death begins to make more sense when we learn to befriend (rather than control) the great paradox of creation-and-destruction. Millions are not even aware of the paradox, and we cannot befriend that which we don't consciously embrace.

Awareness is the beginning of discernment, and particularly the acknowledgment that we humans learn to engage wisely when we make ourselves transparent to the foundational wisdom of creation itself. On a cosmic and planetary scale, death has flourished for several billions of years, right from that earliest time when matter and anti-matter did their primordial double-edged dance, to be followed by violent explosions within stars leading in time to the formation of galaxies, the oxygen crisis that gave birth to our capacity for respiration, and the evolution of heterotrophy in which organisms began to feed off one another. Sacrifice is written into every dimension of creation's story. Colloquially, the word denotes "giving something up," but paradoxically it also means making something sacred.[16]

In the contemporary world we need to distinguish between death as an organic dimension of all living systems, and the meaningless suffering accompanying death which baffles humans particularly. On closer examination, it becomes clear that most of the meaningless suffering associated with death, and pertaining to human fragility, is actually caused by humans themselves. And the primary cause is our wrong modes of intervening in nature's processes. At the heart of those inappropriate, irresponsible interventions is the human addiction to power and control. Our insatiable desire to be totally in charge is the root cause of most of the meaningless suffering in the world.

If humans could withdraw, or, in the first place, withhold, all their wrong interventions, the plight of pain and suffering in the world would be substantially altered and reduced. There would still be pain, suffering, and death. We would still witness freaks of nature like storms and hurricanes. The difference would be in our mode of understanding: we would be more intuitively evolved to see these destructive elements as inherent and necessary to evolution's forward movement. Of course, in that altered state of perception and consciousness, some death-dealing illnesses that exist today, e.g., cancer and coronary problems, would probably be reduced considerably. Many of our worst illnesses are directly linked to our most irrational fears, particularly to the compulsive need for domination and control. We bring on ourselves the very things we fear most.

The Dynamics of Death — and of Life!

Generally speaking, nobody looks forward to dying; in truth, most of us dread the thought of it. By the same token, none of us likes anything to do with decline or diminishment, in self, others, or the institutions in which we have invested our life's energies. Letting-go is an acclaimed Christian ascetical virtue, but not in much demand. Instead we cling on as much as possible — and for as long as possible. Ideally we would like to live forever, and in the absence of that possibility on earth, we have projected it onto the life hereafter. A consoling prospect, but not one that empowers us to deal with death (or with life) in a more creative and constructive way.

Elisabeth Kübler-Ross (1970; 1982) is a leading authority on the psychology of death and dying. She has closely observed and systematically analyzed people's responses at different stages in the dying process. Similarly for those grieving the loss of loved ones: they too go through a range of experiences quite similar to those confronting an imminent death.

More intriguing still is the application of those same insights to what happens when major institutions begin to decline and face possible termination. People directly involved go into defense mode, frequently into utter denial, and can be seen to live out of the same stages as those identified by Kübler-Ross. There is one notable difference in the case of institutional decline and death: the defensive responses are much more subtle and often governed by a group sub-consciousness rather than by an individual response. In the case of the group, the subconscious motivation is much deeper and may take much longer to bring it into conscious awareness. Group or systemic resistance is always more difficult to confront and break down. The thought of possible disintegration is just too much to acknowledge.

In what is now regarded as a classic piece of research, Kübler-Ross has identified five stages characteristic of people facing their own death. These stages of the dying process are reminiscent of what we experience every time we have to deal with significant loss — in our personal or collective lives:

1. Denial

"This can't be happening to me!" We don't want to know and will go to great lengths to rationalize the impending sense of loss. For at least some time we will try to pretend that everything is as it was before. The denial is all the more intransigent if it is rooted in the pain of past losses that have never been dealt with. We can't embrace the here-and-now because our defenses are locked into painful past memories. The ensuing stress on loved ones can be quite distressing, since all attempts at caring are likely to be rebuffed.

Denial as an adult personal response is widely reinforced by the cultural norms of contemporary society. We must put on a brave face; to be vulnerable is to be weak and that is unacceptable. We invoke the metaphor of the lone warrior, and what a deadly lonely place it can be at times.

The collective denial thrives on similar dynamics except that they can be much more subtle and resistant to becoming conscious. An organization may have outlived its usefulness and relevance, but we can't let go; to the contrary, we cling on more rigidly than ever. Religious organizations have the added weight of tradition and ide-ology — that which belongs to God must never die out! Precisely at this juncture the organization begins to lose the faith and allegiance of its rank-and-file members. People of more adult maturity move out — and try to move on. Sometimes, this can be a costly move, but personal integrity requires what to others may seem like a drastic option, even a betrayal. And for those remaining behind, this can deepen their sense of denial, which then is likely to move rapidly into Kübler-Ross's second stage: anger.

Currently, as a human species we are dangerously locked into various rigid denials. Life on planet earth is severely strained by humanly created threats. Currently, global warming is to the fore, resulting in rapidly rising sea levels likely to submerge many islands and some cities within the next few decades. And as global warming creates almost weekly scare headlines, we tend to underestimate the enormity of other threats: serious deterioration in the quality of air and water, excessive removal of topsoil, extinction of species, warfare, poverty, and the ruthless exploitation pioneered by megacorporations. Politicians, economists, and policy-makers continue to ignore the ominous signs. Governments all over the world adhere to patriarchal forms of governance, clinging to an ideology that is rapidly becoming anachronistic. And huge sectors of society, especially the youth, instead of facing the dysfunctional mess in which we find ourselves as a civilization, escape into the nebulous world of popular music, drugs and hedonistic behavior. Denial is a major cultural block, and not an easy one to confront.

2. Anger

Fortunately the resistance of denial tends to weaken after some time, and the energy of anger begins to surface. The anger may be with self, with life, with doctors, possibly with God. Handled creatively, this can be quite a liberating moment, but rarely is this possible. Anger is itself an emotion that our culture holds in strong denial: people who are in control of their lives (and their emotions) should not be angry! We don't like anger, so we have developed a whole series of cultural responses whereby we quickly repress it.

Anger is an incredibly creative and liberating emotion, but its expression tends to be messy and untidy. And because we are so uncomfortable with it as an emotion, as a species we are not skilled to embrace it constructively and confront it appropriately. Our culture therefore tends to mishandle anger in two extreme ways: repress it out of existence, which in the long term creates even more dangerous consequences, or project it unreflectively onto various societal scapegoats, authority figures being the typical target. Being at home with our anger and learning to befriend it in a creative and constructive way is probably one of the most urgent challenges of our time, one that every mature adult needs to embrace in order to live meaningfully in these difficult times.

The anger that relates to the death experience tends to be the type that goes nowhere. It is often internalized and quickly changes to a sense of moodiness, withdrawal, or depression. Friends and relatives try to lighten the atmosphere, often unaware of what is going on in the inner realm of the soul. Sometimes the anger is spiritualized in a way that complicates rather than adds meaning to the fear of death or the sense of loss. Pastorally, we are often in the dilemma of not knowing what to do with anger.

In the collective realm, anger quickly runs in pursuit of scapegoats. Those within the organization are likely to be marginalized, demoted, and ridiculed. In extreme cases, they may be expelled, and then the attention will shift to external scapegoats, which may be those conjuring up new "heretical" ideas or those whose influence is perceived as malicious and dangerous. Every attempt is being made to stop the organization looking at its own internal malaise. That is a truth that the group is not ready to confront, a truth that can be faced only if and when the group learns to acknowledge and befriend its own anger.

3. Bargaining

This is the juncture at which the person faced with terminal illness memorizes a number of well-known scripts: If I give up drinking...; If I become a vegetarian...; If I exercise regularly...; If I cling to just one partner...; If I go back to church..., perhaps, I will be granted a reprieve! It can also involve an internal ritual of promises to self or to God: If I am spared I'll give my wealth to charity; I'll do voluntary overseas work, etc. Often these thoughts remain internal, and may not even be consciously recognized by the person herself. They evolve more as fantasies but ones that can be hugely significant in advancing the process of facing death or sustained loss.

Here we encounter that feature of the contemporary world where everything is valued in terms of a price. And to get the best value we must bargain for it. It is a control game, one that helps us remain sane in this rather crazy consumerist culture that we have invented. In collective terms, it is often encapsulated in the image of shifting around the deck chairs hoping to rebalance a ship that is already sinking. In religious orders we convince ourselves that if we pray hard enough for vocations, new members will eventually come our way and then we won't have to sacrifice any of our major institutions. Bargaining keeps the inevitable at bay, till eventually the psychic energy is spun out, and then depression is inescapable.

4. Depression

When all the human efforts fail (the denial, the anger, the bargaining), provided of course that we have not become stuck at one or another stage, then we come face to face with the inevitable. We feel helpless, listless, de-energized. The control games of patriarchy, which have sustained us perhaps over an entire lifetime, don't work anymore. We may be among the fortunate ones who learned during life — often through trauma or breakdown — to let go and let God! Only a minority of us are likely to have had that paradoxically blessed experience.

Depression has been described as *a learned sense of helplessness.* The strategies of being able to control a situation don't work anymore, and therefore there is nothing we can do. We are totally helpless — not because the situation itself leaves us that way, but because of the enculturation we inherited from the society in which we lived. We have been indoctrinated into the notion that we must be in charge of what is happening to us. And when we no longer are, we are left with a frightening sense of paralysis, not knowing what to do. That, in many cases, is what depression is about.

Elisabeth Kübler-Ross speaks of *reactive* and *preparatory* depression. Institutions and organizations tend to get stuck in the reactive mode, frequently spiraling back to the anger stage. If individuals have a healthy network of peers and/or loved ones, they can move more easily through the depressive feelings and begin more direct engagement with the issues at hand. This is the beginning of the acceptance, and the new hope it can offer to all concerned.

5. Acceptance

Acceptance is not just a cold sense of resignation, which it would be if the other stages had not been negotiated. This is something akin to the mystical clarity that ensues after the mystical dark night of sense and soul (see Moore 2004). The person may be sad, angry and confused at times, and so will relatives and loved ones. But there is a sense of proactive engagement. Finances need to be sorted out; loved ones need to be cared for. Final duties need to be dispensed, and, not uncommonly, the dying person wants to be involved in planning her own funeral.

When this final stage is negotiated with dignity and transparency it certainly enables the suffering or dying person to reclaim a sense of dignity and peace, but equally important it leaves loved ones with an enormous sense of wholeness and truth. There is nothing more painful than to see people in meaningless pain and agonizing suffering. Conversely, there is no greater gift we can leave our loved ones than the gift of dying well, a controversial issue in modern times as more people seek to have a say in their own dying, especially when confronted with the wasting and painful conditions of a terminal illness.[17]

Institutionally, we don't have much "good practice" to illustrate the significance of this last stage. Organizations rarely reach a final moment of death; they have been folded up, often by the bank to which they owed so much money, or they have been absorbed into another enterprise. There was no proper ending, and a lot of people prefer it that way. We don't like endings and are very ill equipped at dealing with them creatively and constructively.

The five stages developed by Kübler-Ross, and endorsed by many colleagues, teach us a great deal about the adult at work in an engaged, proactive, and creative way. The adult does not dodge or sidestep challenges, not even the complex enterprise of death and dying, whether personally or institutionally. And I am not alluding merely to death. Handling these stages of death and dying in a wholesome and informed way illuminates many of the dynamics that generate healthy adulthood. In fact, adults will handle this material well only if they have already handled well other life crises that they have encountered. From the perspective of adult faith in the twenty-first century, life and death are perceived as handmaids; we cannot embrace the one without becoming well acquainted with the other.

Letting Go into Deeper Freedom

All the major religions reinforce the great paradox of losing one's life to find it anew. It makes no logical sense, yet intuitively and experientially we know it holds truth. The sacrifices of life can make us embittered or compassionate. It very much depends who has been there with us and for us as we face the losses, big and small.

The personal journey through death is the final enactment of an experience we have been through many times. Because of life's circumstances, or the natural slowing down brought on by age and depleting energy, every person encounters the experience of having to let go. It is salutary to learn the wisdom of letting go rather than continuously battling it out forever striving to be a winner, which is often a subconscious fear of losing control. By embracing letting go in a more wholesome way we become compassionate, caring, and more at peace with our paradoxical universe.

We are also likely to engage more creatively with the process of letting go when we are not fretful and frightened about questions of ultimate destiny. The monotheistic religions promise enduring life after death — for weal or for woe. The great Eastern religions favor a more cyclic resolution in the process of reincarnation. Both theories are intended to provide reassurance and hope. Many take the theories at their face value; people of adult faith often seek other explanations.

I find the insights of modern science to be both helpful and informative. We know that energy is the life-stuff that animates and sustains everything in creation. We know that energy is never wasted, but always transformed into alternative uses. We also know that creation recycles on an enormous scale, ensuring that nothing is ever wasted. And theologically, we believe that the Holy Spirit of God is the life force within and behind this energy-process.

The energy that constitutes my individual self is dissolved in death and returns to the great energy fields of creation, whence it originated in the first place. The core of my individuality is recycled in the great melting pot of creation's becoming. My individual energy has been transformed into cosmic potentialities about which the human rational mind knows nothing. And my individual destiny from there on, along with that of all the loved ones gone before me, is in the hands of a wisdom greater than ours.

Whether or not I will be reunited with loved ones in the afterlife, is no longer the real issue. (I acknowledge it is hugely important for many people.) The real issue is one of trust, the great antidote to power. Do I trust the fundamental creativity of evolution? The wisdom of a universe that far outstretches human knowledge? The great embracing mystery that defies and ultimately supersedes all our yearnings for certainty? The cloud of unknowing where all is known? This is where adult faith reaches its apex. The mystics call it *divine abandonment.*

Patriarchal cultures (and religions) dread words like "abandonment" and "surrender." Yet it is in the radical trust of such letting go that we embrace a kind of ultimate freedom, which science on the one hand and emerging spirituality on the other, identify as a creative destiny awaiting all organic life, human and otherwise. We cannot rationally prove this, and for faithful adults of the twenty-first century the cult of rationality is wearing thin. Our trust, our hope and our faith are lured in the direction of enlarged horizons. We are becoming much more aware of the universe we inhabit, the dynamic and resilient web of life, sustaining and transforming our every endeavor, including the trajectory of death itself.

There are no final answers, but the questions endure with a pervasive ring of truth, the driving force of evolution itself!

(a) **Conventional inherited wisdom** *is built around a petrified sense of both life and death, viewing death as a final judgment leading to happiness or ruination in a life beyond the present creation.*

(b) **Embedded codependency** *uses the fear of death and the prospect of eternal doom as a way of keeping people feeling unworthy, fearful, and therefore easier to control.*

(c) **Adult empowerment** *means seeing and understanding death as a necessary transformative dynamic that permeates life at every level. Next, we need to become more aware of how meaningless we make death by so much fear and denial. Finally, we need to see our personal deaths as a transformative reconnection with the great energy fields of God's creation.*

Notes

1. According to Transactional Analysis (TA), there are three ego-states that people consistently employ:

- **Parent:** a state in which people behave, feel, and think in response to an unconscious mimicking of how their parents (or other parental figures) acted, or how they interpreted their parent's actions. For example, a person may shout at someone out of frustration because that person learned from an influential figure in childhood the lesson that this seemed to be an effective way of gaining people's attention.

- **Adult:** a state of mature and integrated self-reliance, relating openly and fearlessly with others, devoid of unhealthy compliance. Learning to strengthen the adult is a goal of TA. When people are in the adult ego state, they are directed toward an objective appraisal of reality.

- **Child:** a state in which people behave, feel, and think similarly to how they did in childhood. For example, a person who receives a poor evaluation at work may respond by looking at the floor and crying or pouting, as they used to when scolded as a child. Conversely, a person who receives a good evaluation may respond with a broad smile and a joyful gesture of thanks in order to earn further approval. The child is the source of emotions, creation, recreation, spontaneity, and intimacy.

Three popular names in the recent development and exposition of Transactional Analysis are those of Eric Berne, Thomas Harris, and Claude Steiner; for a comprehensive overview see Widdowson (2009). And these destructive behaviors are often reinforced in societal institutions such as schools, hospitals, workplaces, and religious organizations.

2. Internalized oppression can be understood in both systemic and personal terms. The political regime of Robert Mugabe in Zimbabwe as evidenced in the opening years of the twenty-first century highlights the systemic mimicry often noted in postcolonial studies. Having thrown off the imposing control of the external colonizer (the British), Robert Mugabe and his cronies have internalized the very domination they fought so hard to get rid of and now impose on the Zimbabwean people forms of oppression and deprivation some of which are worse than the British ever imposed. The personal nature of internalized oppression is often illustrated in how women deal with male power and domination to which they have been subjected over many years. In their attempt to free themselves from such domination, they sometimes begin imposing it on others (men and women) with a vehemence and cruelty far in excess of what they experienced themselves (see Mullaly 2010; *http://web2.uvcs.uvic.ca/courses/csafety/mod2/glossary.htm.*)

3. We note that scholars such as J. Baird Callicott (1991), Wes Jackson (1987), and Jay B. McDaniel (1995) all situate the notion of original sin in the context of the agricultural revolution and not as a deficiency that existed since the dawn of time.

4. It is possible to identify the burgeoning anti-establishment movements of the 1960s as the constituting event of *postmodernism*. In 1971, the Arab-American theorist Ihab Hassan (*The Dismemberment of Orpheus: Toward a Postmodern Literature*) was one of the first to use the term in its present form (although others like Charles Olson had used the term to describe emerging literary trends). Hassan traces the development of what he called "literature of silence" through the Marquis de Sade, Franz Kafka, Ernest Hemingway, Samuel Beckett, and many others, including developments such as the Theater of the Absurd and the *nouveau roman*. In 1979, Jean-François Lyotard wrote a short but influential work, *The Postmodern Condition: A Report on Knowledge*. Richard Rorty wrote *Philosophy and the Mirror of Nature* (1979). Jean Baudrillard, Michel Foucault, and Roland Barthes have all contributed significantly to our contemporary understanding of postmodernism.

For many in the academic domain, postmodernism is the favored analysis of the social, economic, and religious problems confronting the modern world. I tend to view postmodernism as *a consequence* rather than *a cause* of many of the symptoms under assessment. It helps to explain the amorphous destabilizations of our time, using a rather heady analysis not easily connected with the experience of daily life.

5. Frequently throughout the book, I use the word "discernment." In spiritual and theological terms, discernment denotes a desire to be open to divine influence as in attending to the inspiration of the Spirit, or trying to listen more attentively to what God is asking, particularly in the search for spiritual meaning. However, true discernment involves not merely the spiritual and intellectual faculties, but every dimension of our human engagement with life. One commentator concludes his overview with the following guidelines: rooted in community; regular contact with poor and suffering people; daily prayer and contemplation; regular community worship; spiritual accompaniment; a simple lifestyle; physical exercise and a moderate concern for health; regular rest and recreation; study, especially of social reality; a sense of humor (Brackley 2004, 254–55). Other useful references include Caplan (2009), Lowney (2009), and the inspiring autobiography of Patricia Panahi (2008).

6. A vast literature exists on quantum mechanics and the ensuing worldview, popularly known as the quantum worldview. Kenneth Ford (2005), Dean Radin (2006), Marcus Chown (2007) all provide useful and readable overviews.

7. In earlier times, spiritual masters described this as the process of "divine abandonment," citing Jean Pierre Caussade's *Self-Abandonment to Divine Providence* as a classic text. The message of this spiritual classic is often summarized in the words of St. Benedict: "Truly seek God," which can also be rendered: "Truly trust God." "Surrender" is the word more commonly used today to promote this kind of spirituality, one popularized in our time by many adaptations of the twelve-step program, initially used by Alcoholics Anonymous. A number of contemporary spiritual writers strive to integrate the earlier spirituality of abandonment with the contemporary notion of trusting the process of evolution, e.g., Epstein (2005), Gordon (2009), Tarrant (1998).

8. On this topic, Jack Mezirow (2000) is the most frequently cited authority. His approach is often criticized because it is very much based on how individuals learn, and it gives minimal attention to collective, communal processes, nor does

it include the spiritual dimension. The interactive, communal context is deemed to be an essential defining characteristic by several other theorists including Cranton (2006); King (2005); O'Sullivan (2002); Tisdell (2003); a fine summary is available in Stein and Farmer (2004).

9. Initially, the rich evocation of this term is rooted in A. N. Whitehead's process theology, made accessible through authors such as John Cobb and David Griffin (1976), Carol Christ (2003), Catherine Keller (2008). John F. Haught, in several key writings, adopts the concept of *the lure of the future* to illuminate the trust of cosmic, planetary and human evolution. From a Darwinian perspective, we can argue that evolution is driven from the past; at best that is only a partial explanation with the lure of the future providing a much greater impetus for evolutionary becoming: "Anticipation is what bears the universe along as it reaches out toward fuller being" (Haught 2006, 137).

10. In their popular book, *The First Paul,* Marcus Borg and John Dominic Crossan (2009, 124) highlight that St. Paul's understanding of salvation envisages a more just, nonviolent, and empowering way of engaging with life *here on earth* and not some panacea to be obtained in a life hereafter.

11. According to a groundbreaking work by two American feminist scholars, Brock and Parker (2008, 60ff), the imagery in the Roman catacombs displays no portrayals of a judgmental God seeking propitiation through the sufferings of the martyrs. Instead, they suggest that the martyrs envisaged their torture and death as a means of helping to bring about paradise *on this earth* as a place where justice and peace could prevail. In other words, they did not envisage their martyrdom as a means of escaping from this sinful world to the place of ultimate holiness in a world beyond.

12. It is noteworthy that many people in the United States, Canada, and Europe identify rather easily with the universe story of 13.7 billion and the earth story of 3.8 billion. Intuitively those dates make some sense, and many people struggle on how best to integrate this new awareness into their value systems both religiously and culturally. However, when it comes to our great human story — of 7 million years — people seem quite baffled. Some wonder why they have never been told this in the various formative stages of upbringing and education. For others, it seems to be a truth almost too intimate to have to grapple with; it may imply personal and cultural changes the outcomes of which seem uncertain and unpredictable.

13. Contemporary Christian philosophers and theologians seem to consider the views of René Girard (1977; 1986) to be particularly insightful on the emergence and prevalence of human violence. Girard adopts an exclusive anthropocentric approach, deeming violence to be innate to human nature as part of a mimetic learning process. The scholarly appeal of this insight may be related to its novel potential to make sense of the notion of a fundamental flaw, but more importantly its claim that the mimetic violence and its accompanying victimization are finally nullified in the death and resurrection of the Christian Jesus. I disagree primarily with Girard's anthropology, all of which seems to be based on evidence gleaned merely from the past five to seven thousand years. The evidence is highly selective and fails to do justice to the larger, more complex history of human emergence, much of which provides little justification for innate human violence.

14. Thanks to the wider availability of information (via the Internet, etc.), many people detect political spin more easily, and can discern more readily what is mere waffle and what is truth. Among young people in particular this results in a growing sense of cynicism around major institutions, including those pertaining to national governance. Momentarily, we got a glimpse into the sinister nature of the politicoeconomic world in September 2008, when the U.S. government suggested a 700-billion-dollar bailout for failing (or failed?) economic institutions in the United States. Among rank-and-file citizens the anger was palpable as thousands realized that the institutions to which they entrusted their money and financial security had been recklessly trading their trust and resources. And instead of calling the institutions to accountability and transparency, the taxpayers of the nation were being asked to fund the bailout. Those with already scarce resources were expected to rescue the economics of scarcity!

15. To complete the historical picture: in July 1944, the Bretton Woods Agreement, involving forty-five countries, agreed to align all currencies with the U.S. dollar, while retaining gold as the basic unit of value (initially adopted in Britain, in 1720, and later in Germany, in 1871). In 1971, Richard Nixon disconnected the dollar from gold, making the dollar dependent on "floating exchanges" of the international markets. The American dollar still dominates the financial landscape, although the Chinese yuan and the European euro are fast catching up.

16. In an oft-cited work, Nancy Jay (1992) highlights how the concept of sacrifice has been enculturated and spiritualized, predominantly by men, and used as a device to exert dominance and control over nature and over women in particular. "Sacrificial traditions," she writes, "have rarely been questioned about the ways they are grounded in the social relations of reproduction or about the ways they work to achieve male domination" (147).

17. The pros and cons of assisted dying have not been examined in great depth. People who seek such a choice and opt for such an outcome seem to be people of moral integrity, exercising what seems to be adult discernment arising from a genuine love for life and its meaning. Many of the key issues are reviewed with insight and sensitivity by John Spong (2009, 213–27).

Bibliography

Amato, Joseph A. 1990. *Victims and Values: History and a Theory of Suffering*. New York: Praeger.

Anderson, Walter T. 2004. *All Connected Now: Life in the First Global Civilization*. Bellevue, Tenn.: Westview Press.

Avis, Paul. 1990. *Eros and the Sacred*. London: Morehouse.

Beattie, Melody. 1987. *Beyond Codependency: And Getting Better All the Time*. Center City, Minn.: Hazelden.

———. 2009. *The New Codependency: Help and Guidance for Today's Generation*. New York: Simon & Schuster.

Becker, Ernest. 1971. *The Birth and Death of Meaning: An Interdisciplinary Perspective on the Problem of Man*. New York: Free Press.

Berry, Thomas, Mary Evelyn Tucker, and John Grim. 2009. *The Christian Future and the Fate of the Earth*. Maryknoll, N.Y.: Orbis Books.

Bhabha, Homi. 1994. *The Location of Culture*. New York: Routledge.

Black, Peter. 2003. "The Broken Wings of Eros." *Theological Studies* 64: 106–26.

Blatterer, Harry. 2007. "Contemporary Adulthood: Reconceptualizing an Uncontested Category." *Current Sociology* 55: 771–92.

Borg, Marcus, and John D. Crossan. 2009. *The First Paul: Reclaiming the Radical Visionary behind the Church's Conservative Icon*. New York: HarperCollins.

Brackley, Dean. 2004. *The Call to Discernment in Troubled Times: New Perspectives on the Transformative Wisdom of Ignatius of Loyola*. New York: Crossroad.

Brock, Rita Nakashima, and Rebecca Parker. 2008. *Saving Paradise: How Christianity Traded Love of This World for Crucifixion and Empire*. Boston: Beacon Press.

Brueggemann, Walter. 1986. *Hopeful Imagination: Prophetic Voices in Exile*. Philadelphia: Fortress.

Callicott, J. Baird. 1991. *In Defense of the Land Ethic: Essays in Environmental Philosophy*. Albany: State University of New York Press.

Cannato, Judy. 2006. *Radical Amazement: Contemplative Lessons from Black Holes, Supernovas, and Other Wonders of the Universe*. Notre Dame, Ind.: Sorin Books.

———. 2010. *Field of Compassion*. Notre Dame, Ind.: Sorin Books.

Caplan, Mariana. 2009. *Eyes Wide Open: Cultivating Discernment on the Spiritual Path*. Boulder, Colo.: Sounds True.

Capra, Fritjof. 2002. *The Hidden Connections*. London: HarperCollins.

Carrette, Jeremy, and Richard King. 2005. *Selling Spirituality: The Silent Takeover of Religion*. New York: Routledge.

Carter, Rita. 2008. *Multiplicity: The New Science of Personality*. London: Little Brown.

Cavanagh, John, ed. 2002. *Alternatives to Economic Globalization: A Better World Is Possible*. San Francisco: Berrett-Koehler.

Chalmers, D. J. 1996. *The Conscious Mind: In Search of a Fundamental Theory.* New York: Oxford University Press.

Chown, Marcus. 2007. *Quantum Theory Cannot Hurt You: A Guide to the Universe.* London: Faber & Faber.

Christ, Carol. 2003. *She Who Changes: Re-Imagining the Divine in the World.* New York: Palgrave Macmillan.

Clayton, Philip, and Paul Davies. 2006. *The Re-emergence of Emergence: The Emergentist Hypothesis from Science to Religion.* Oxford and New York: Oxford University Press.

Cobb, John, and David R. Griffin. 1976. *Process Theology: An Introductory Exposition.* Philadelphia: Westminster Press.

Cook-Greuter, Susanne R., and Melvin E. Miller. 1994. *Transcendence and Mature Thought in Adulthood: The Further Reaches of Adult Development.* Lanham, Md.: Rowman & Littlefield.

———. 1999. *Creativity, Spirituality, and Transcendence: Paths to Integrity and Wisdom in the Mature Self.* Stamford, Conn.: Ablex Publishing.

Corr, Charles A. 2008. *Death and Dying: Life and Living.* Florence, Ky.: Wadsworth Publishing.

Cranton, Patricia. 2006. *Understanding and Promoting Transformative Learning: A Guide for Educators of Adults.* San Francisco: Jossey-Bass.

Crockett, William R. 1989. *Eucharist: Symbol of Transformation.* New York: Pueblo.

Crossan, John Dominic. 2007. *God and Empire: Jesus against Rome, Then and Now.* San Francisco: HarperSanFrancisco.

———, and Richard Watts. 1996. *Who Is Jesus? Answers to Your Questions about the Historical Jesus.* Louisville: Westminster John Knox Press.

Delio, Ilia. 2008. *Christ in Evolution.* Maryknoll, N.Y.: Orbis Books.

Dennett, Daniel. 1993. *Consciousness Explained.* New York: Penguin.

De Sousa, Ronald. 2007. *Why Think? The Evolution of the Rational Mind.* Oxford: Oxford University Press.

De Waal, Frans. 2005. *Our Inner Ape: The Best and the Worst in Human Nature.* New York: Penguin.

Donovan, Vincent J. 1989. *The Church in the Midst of Creation.* Maryknoll, N.Y.: Orbis Books.

Dowd, Michael. 2008. *Thank God for Evolution.* New York: Plume/Penguin.

Dryzek, John S. 1987. *Rational Ecology: Environment and Political Economy.* New York: Wiley.

Epstein, Mark. 2005. *Open to Desire: The Truth about What the Buddha Taught.* New York: Gotham Books.

Epstein, Robert. 2007. *The Case against Adolescence: Rediscovering the Adult in Every Teen.* Fresno, Calif.: Quill Driver.

Farley, Margaret A. 2008. *Just Love: A Framework for Christian Sexual Ethics.* New York: Continuum.

Fiese, B. H., and D. J. Scaturo. 1995. "The Use of Self-Help Terminology in Focus-Group Discussions with Adult Children of Alcoholics: Implications for Research and Clinical Practice." *Family Therapy* 22, no. 1: 1–8.

Ford, Kenneth. 2005. *The Quantum World: Quantum Physics for Everyone.* Cambridge, Mass.: Harvard University Press.

Foster, Charles. 2009. *The Selfless Gene: Living with God and Darwin.* Nashville: Thomas Nelson.

Fowler, James. 1982. *Stages of Faith: The Psychology of Human Development and the Quest for Meaning.* New York: Harper & Row.

Francis, Leslie J., and Jeff Astley. 1992. *Christian Perspectives on Faith Development.* Leominster, UK: Gracewing.

Fry, Douglas P., and Kaj Bjorkqvist. 1997. *Cultural Variation in Conflict Resolution: Alternatives to Violence.* Philadelphia: Lawrence Erlbaum Publishers.

Girard, René. 1977. *Violence and the Sacred.* Baltimore: Johns Hopkins University Press.

———. 1986. *The Scapegoat.* Baltimore: Johns Hopkins University Press.

Goodall, Jane. 1986. *The Chimpanzees of Gombe: Patterns of Behavior.* Cambridge, Mass.: Harvard University Press.

———. 2001. *My Life with Chimpanzees.* New York: Time Warner Audio Books.

Gordon, Gus. 2009. *Solitude and Compassion: The Path to the Heart of the Gospel.* Maryknoll, N.Y.: Orbis Books.

Hand, Judith L. 2003. *Women, Power and the Biology of Peace.* San Diego: Questpath Publishing.

Hart, Donna, and Robert W. Sussman. 2005. *Man the Hunted: Primates, Predators, and Human Evolution.* New York: Basic Books.

Hathaway, Mark, and Leonardo Boff. 2009. *The Tao of Liberation: Exploring the Ecology of Transformation.* Maryknoll, N.Y.: Orbis Books.

Haught, John F. 2006. *Is Nature Enough?* New York: Cambridge University Press.

Hawken, Paul. 2007. *Blessed Unrest: How the Largest Movement in the World Came into Being, and Why No One Saw It Coming.* New York: Penguin/Viking.

Heelas, Paul. 2008. *Spiritualities of Life: New Age Romanticism and Consumptive Capitalism.* Oxford: Blackwell.

Heyward, Carter. 1989. *Touching Our Strength: The Erotic as Power and the Love of God.* San Francisco: HarperSanFrancisco.

Hill, Jason. 2002. *On Being a Cosmopolitan: What It Means to Be Human.* Lanham, Md.: Rowman & Littlefield.

———. 2009. *Beyond Blood Identities: Post-humanity in the Twenty-First Century.* Lanham, Md.: Rowman & Littlefield.

Hrdy, Sarah Blaffer. 2009. *Mothers and Others: The Evolutionary Origins of Mutual Understanding.* Cambridge, Mass.: Harvard University Press.

Jackson, Wes. 1987. *Meeting the Expectations of the Land: Essays in Sustainable Agriculture and Stewardship.* New York: Farrar, Straus & Giroux.

Jay, Nancy. 1992. *Throughout Your Generations Forever: Sacrifice, Religion, and Paternity.* Chicago: University of Chicago Press.

Jordan, Mark D. 2000. *The Silence of Sodom: Homosexuality in Modern Catholicism.* Chicago: University of Chicago Press.

Keen, Sam. 1985. *The Passionate Life: Stages of Loving.* New York: Harper.

Keller, Catherine. 2008. *On the Mystery: Discerning Divinity in Process.* Minneapolis: Fortress.

Kennedy, Alan. 1974. *Protean Self: Dramatic Action in Contemporary Fiction.* London: Macmillan.

King, Kathleen P. 2005. *Bringing Transformative Learning to Life.* Malabar, Fla.: Krieger.

King, Ursula. 2009. *The Search for Spirituality: Our Global Quest for a Spiritual Life*. Norwich, UK: Canterbury Press.

Korten, David C. 2006. *The Great Turning: From Empire to Earth Community*. San Francisco: Berrett-Koehler.

Kübler-Ross, Elisabeth. 1970. *On Death and Dying*. New York: Methuen.

———. 1982. *Living with Death and Dying*. London: Souvenir Press.

Laitin, David. 2007. *Nations, States, and Violence*. Oxford: Oxford University Press.

Lanzetta, Beverly J. 2005. *Radical Wisdom: A Feminist Mystical Theology*. Minneapolis: Fortress Press.

Laszlo, Ervin. 1996. *Evolution: The General Theory*. Gresskill, N.J.: Hampton Press.

Lee, R. B. 1979. *The Kung San: Men, Women, and Work in a Foraging Society*. Cambridge: Cambridge University Press.

Lewis, C. S. 1960. *The Four Loves*. New York: Harcourt Brace.

Lietaer, Bernard. 2001. *The Future of Money: A New Way to Create Wealth, Work and a Wiser World*. London: Random House.

Lifton, Robert J. 1999. *The Protean Self: Human Resilience in an Age of Fragmentation*. Chicago: University of Chicago Press.

Lorde, Audre. 1984, 2007. *Sister Outsider: Essays and Speeches*. New York: Crown Publishing/Crossing Press.

Lowney, Chris. 2009. *Heroic Living: Discover Your Purpose and Change the World*. Chicago: Loyola Press.

Lynch, Gordon. 2007. *New Spirituality: An Introduction to Belief Beyond Religion*. London: I. B. Taurus.

Margulis, Lynn. 1998. *The Symbiotic Planet*. New York: Basic Books.

McDaniel, Jay B. 1995. *With Roots and Wings: Christianity in an Age of Ecology and Dialogue*. Maryknoll, N.Y.: Orbis Books.

McFague, Sallie. 2001. *Life Abundant: Rethinking Theology and Economy for a Planet in Peril*. Minneapolis: Fortress Press.

Mezirow, J. 2000. *Learning as Transformation: Critical Perspectives on a Theory in Progress*. San Francisco: Jossey Bass.

Moore, Thomas. 2004. *Dark Nights of the Soul: A Guide to Finding Your Way through Life's Ordeals*. San Francisco: HarperSanFrancisco.

Morowitz, Harold J. 2002. *The Emergence of Everything: How the World Became Complex*. Oxford and New York: Oxford University Press.

Mullaly, Bob. 2010. *Challenging Oppression and Confronting Privilege: A Critical Social Work Approach*. New York: Oxford University Press.

Neiman, Susan. 2009. *Moral Clarity: A Guide for Grown-up Idealists*. New York: Random House.

Nussbaum, Martha C. 2001. *Women and Human Development: The Capabilities Approach*. New York: Cambridge University Press.

———. 2007. *Frontiers of Justice: Disability, Nationality, Species Membership*. Cambridge, Mass.: Harvard University Press.

Nygren, Anders. 1983. *Agape and Eros*. London: SPCK.

Ohmae, Kenichi. 2005. *The Next Global Stage: Challenges and Opportunities in Our Borderless World*. Columbus, Ohio: McGraw-Hill.

O'Murchu, Diarmuid. 1998. *Reclaiming Spirituality: A New Spiritual Framework for Today's World*. New York: Crossroad.

————. 2008. *Ancestral Grace: Meeting God in Our Human Story.* Maryknoll, N.Y.: Orbis Books.

————. 2009. *Jesus in the Power of Poetry: A New Voice for Gospel Truth.* New York: Crossroad.

O'Sullivan, Edmund, et al. 2002. *Expanding the Boundaries of Transformative Learning: Essays on Theory and Praxis.* New York: Palgrave.

Panahi, Patricia. 2008. *God outside the Box: A Story of Breaking Free.* Bloomington, Ind.: Authorhouse.

Patterson, Stephen J. 2004. *Beyond the Passion: Rethinking the Death and Life of Jesus.* Minneapolis: Augsburg Fortress.

Pears, Angie. 2009. *Doing Contextual Theology.* London: Routledge.

Pink, Daniel. 2008. *A Whole New Mind: Why Right-Brainers Will Rule the Future.* London: Marshall Cavendish.

Plotkin, Bill. 2008. *www.natureandthehumansoul.com/newbook/aboutBill.htm.*

Plumwood, Val. 2002. *Environmental Culture: The Ecological Crisis of Reason.* New York: Routledge.

Power, Margaret. 1991. *The Egalitarians: Human and Chimpanzee.* Cambridge: Cambridge University Press.

Primack, Joel, and Nancy Abrams. 2007. *The View from the Center of the Universe: Discovering Our Extraordinary Place in the Cosmos.* New York: Riverhead Books.

Radin, Dean. 2006. *Entangled Minds: Extrasensory Experiences in a Quantum Reality.* New York: Pocket Books.

Ralston Saul, John. 1994. *Voltaire's Bastards: The Dictatorship of Reason in the West.* New York: Vintage Books.

Ray, Kathleen Darby. 1998. *Deceiving the Devil: Atonement, Abuse and Ransom.* Cleveland: Pilgrim Press.

Ray, Paul H., and Sherry Ruth Anderson. 2000. *The Cultural Creatives: How 50 Million People Are Changing the World.* New York: Harmony Books.

Rosenberg, Gregg H. 2004. *A Place for Consciousness: Probing the Deep Structure of the Natural World.* New York: Oxford University Press.

Roszak, Theodore. 2001. *The Longevity Revolution.* Berkeley, Calif.: Berkeley Hills Books.

Ruether, Rosemary Radford. 1998. *Women and Redemption: A Theological History.* London: SCM Press.

Said, Edward W. 1993. *Culture and Imperialism.* New York: Vintage.

Saxonhouse, Arlene W. 1988. "The Tyranny of Reason in the World of the Polis." *American Political Science Review* 82: 1261–75

Scaturo, D. J., et al. 2000. "The Concept of Codependency and Its Context within Family Systems Theory." *Family Therapy* 27, no. 2: 63–70.

Segovia, Fernando, and R. S. Sugirtharajah. 2009. *A Postcolonial Commentary on the New Testament Writings.* New York and London: T. & T. Clark.

Sheldrake, Rupert. 2009. *Morphic Resonance: The Nature of Formative Causation.* South Paris, Maine: Park Street Press.

Slee, Nicola. 2004. *Women's Faith Development: Patterns and Processes.* Burlington, Vt.: Ashgate.

Sobrino, Jon. 2004. *Where Is God? Earthquake, Terrorism, Barbarity, and Hope.* Maryknoll, N.Y.: Orbis Books.

Spong, John Shelby. 2009. *Eternal Life: A New Vision*. New York: HarperOne.

Starker, Steven. 2002. *Oracle at the Supermarket: The American Preoccupation with Self-Help Books*. Edison, N.J.: Transaction Publishers.

Stein, Sue, and Shaman Farmer. 2004. *Connotative Learning: The Trainer's Guide*. Dubuque, Iowa: Kendall Hunt.

Stewart, John. 2000. *Evolution's Arrow: The Direction of Evolution and the Future of Humanity*. Canberra, Australia: Chapman Press.

Strawson, Galen, et al. 2006. *Consciousness and Its Place in Nature: Does Physicalism Entail Panpsychism?* Charlottesville, Va.: Imprint Academic.

Stringer, Chris, and Rob McKie. 1996. *African Exodus: The Origins of Modern Humanity*. London: Holt/Macmillan.

Swimme, Brian, and Thomas Berry. 1992. *The Universe Story: From the Primordial Flaring Forth to the Ecozoic Era — a Celebration of the Unfolding of the Cosmos*. New York: Penguin.

Tacey, David. 2004. *The Spirituality Revolution: The Emergence of Contemporary Spirituality*. New York: Brunner-Routledge.

Tarlow, Mikela and Philip. 2002. *Digital Aboriginal: The Direction of Business Now*. New York: Time Warner Books.

Tarrant, John. 1998. *The Light Inside the Dark: Zen, Soul and the Spiritual Life*. San Francisco: Harper.

Taylor, Steve. 2005. *The Fall: The Evidence for a Golden Age, 6,000 Years of Insanity, and the Dawning of a New Era*. Winchester, UK, and New York: O Books.

Tickerhoof, Bernard. 2002. *Paradox: The Spiritual Path to Transformation*. Mystic, Conn.: Twenty-third Publications.

Tisdell, Elizabeth. 2003. *Exploring Spirituality and Culture in Adult and Higher Education*. San Francisco: John Wiley.

Vigil, José María, et al. 2010. *Toward a Planetary Theology*. Montreal: Dunamis Publishers.

Waters, Brent. 2006. *From Human to Posthuman: Christian Theology and Technology in a Postmodern World*. Burlington, Vt.: Ashgate.

Wheatley, Margaret J. 1992. *Leadership and the New Science: Learning about Organization from An Orderly Universe*. San Francisco: Berrett-Koehler.

Whitehead, James D., and Evelyn E. Whitehead. 2009. *Holy Eros: Recovering the Passion of God*. Maryknoll, N.Y.: Orbis Books.

Widdowson, Mark. 2009. *Transactional Analysis: 100 Key Points and Techniques*. New York: Routledge.

Wilshire, Bruce. 1998. *Wild Hunger: The Primal Roots of Modern Addiction*. Lanham, Md.: Rowman & Littlefield.

Wilson-Schaef, Anne. 1987. *When Society Becomes an Addict*. San Francisco: Harper & Row.

Wink, Walter. 1992. *Engaging the Powers: Discernment and Resistance in a World of Domination*. Minneapolis: Augsburg Fortress.

Winter, Miriam Therese. 2009. *Paradoxology: Spirituality in a Quantum Universe*. Maryknoll, N.Y.: Orbis Books.

Index